THE USE OF PLASTICS MATERIALS IN BUILDING

Prepared by
The Engineering Equipment Users Association

THE USE OF
PLASTICS MATERIALS
IN BUILDING

E.E.U.A. Handbook No. 31: 1973

Published for

THE ENGINEERING EQUIPMENT USERS ASSOCIATION

20 Grosvenor Place, London, SW1X 7HZ

by

CONSTABLE   LONDON

First published in Great Britain 1973
by Constable and Company Ltd.
10 Orange Street, London WC2H 7EG
Copyright © 1973 Engineering Equipment Users Association
ISBN 0 09 458870 8

Text set in 10/11 pt. IBM Press Roman, printed by photolithography,
and bound in Great Britain at The Pitman Press, Bath

THE ENGINEERING EQUIPMENT USERS ASSOCIATION

The Engineering Equipment Users Association is an association of industrial users of engineering equipment, material and stores. It was founded in 1949 by a number of large companies who realised the important role that would be played in the future by the further standardisation and simplification of engineering products, and by the free exchange of technical information on engineering matters.

The principal objects of E.E.U.A. are to assist its members to promote a common policy for the standardisation of engineering materials, equipment and stores through the British Standards Institution or otherwise; to foster the preparation and adoption of national standards for such products and to collate and summarise information in order to give guidance on their nature and use. Membership is restricted to companies and other bodies who are predominantly users rather than manufacturers of engineering products.

The work of the Association is entirely complementary to that of the B.S.I. with whom close liaison and collaboration are always maintained; it does not duplicate the activity of that Institution in any way. Everything possible is done to enlist the early support of manufacturing interests in standardisation work which E.E.U.A. considers should be promoted in the national interest.

This Handbook was prepared by a panel drawn from member companies in order to gather, collate and summarise available data on the use of plastics materials in building, and to prepare a document which would provide guidance on the nature and use of such materials in different building applications. The results of the panel's work are incorporated in the present Handbook, which the E.E.U.A. Council decided should be published for general sale.

ENGINEERING EQUIPMENT USERS ASSOCIATION

THE USE OF PLASTICS MATERIALS IN BUILDING

(E.E.U.A. Handbook No. 31: 1973)

This Handbook was prepared by a E.E.U.A. Panel IB/2 (The Use of Plastics Materials in Building), constituted from representatives of the following member organisations: −

Albright & Wilson Limited
Central Electricity Generating Board
Courtaulds Limited
Dunlop Limited
Imperial Chemical Industries Limited
Shell International Petroleum Company Limited
Unilever Limited
United Kingdom Atomic Energy Authority

FOREWORD

This handbook is a guide to the selection and use of suitable plastics as construction materials in building. During its preparation various methods of presenting the information were considered. One of these was to deal with the various types of plastics and the forms in which they are available and then to describe typical applications, e.g. polyvinyl chloride (PVC), extruded as pipe that can be used to carry water.

To ensure better continuity and ease of reference, however, the information is presented in Sections relating to the various parts of a building or of a construction operation, the application of plastics being described in each instance.

In some applications plastics are now established just as firmly as other traditional materials, and where appropriate, reference is made to the materials and techniques currently in use. New applications are being constantly introduced and some background information is, therefore, provided to help assess the likely performance of new plastics components. Such components may be offered by manufacturers as a result of anticipated economies in construction, shortages of traditional building materials or because of the relatively superior properties of the plastics themselves, etc. Components for buildings are often made from a number of different materials, and in many instances plastics can be used to give other materials properties they do not possess in themselves. References are also made to the use of plastics for such purposes.

Careful consideration was given to terminology or the choice of terms for describing plastics, and those recommended in BS 3502 (Schedule of Common Names and Abbreviations for Plastics and Rubbers) are used whenever possible. It is often difficult, however, to identify a proprietary plastic with the particular materials from which it is made, since trade names often fail to indicate the true nature of the item and also because it is difficult to produce a reliable and useable table of property characteristics. (See Appendix A). Manufacturers are becoming more aware of the need to provide such information and it is hoped that the practice of so doing will become more common; it should be asked for if not provided.

Dimensions and properties are given in SI units though imperial units are given or included in some cases, notably in Section Eight.

It should be clearly understood that references to materials or components that may be associated with particular manufacturers or suppliers does not imply that satisfactory items of a similar nature cannot be obtained from other sources or are not being developed or applied elsewhere. Readers of this Handbook are in no way restricted or discouraged from purchasing or dealing with any particular manufacturer or supplier.

The Association wishes to thank all those who have kindly supplied data and illustrations either directly or to members of the Panel, or who may have helped in other ways.

THE USE OF PLASTICS MATERIALS IN BUILDING

(E.E.U.A. Handbook No. 31)

CONTENTS

PAGE

Foreword

SECTION ONE: INTRODUCTION TO PLASTICS AND RUBBERS   . . .   1

(a) *General Notes on Plastics*   1

(b) *Advantages of Plastics in Building*   1

(c) *Factors Involved in the Use of Plastics*   2

    (i) Dimensional stability – stress rupture   2
    (ii) Colour fastness and weather resistance   2
    (iii) Safety from fire   3
    (iv) Resistance to water and water vapour   4
    (v) Thermal expansion   4
    (vi) Thermal insulation   4
    (vii) Acoustic insulation   4

(d) *The More Important Plastics in Building (and Physical Properties)*   5
    (i) Types of plastics used   5
    (ii) Physical properties   5

(e) *General Note on Rubbers Used in Building*   10

SECTION TWO: ECONOMIC CONSIDERATIONS   13

SECTION THREE: FOUNDATIONS   15

(a) *Introduction*   15

(b) *Plastics Materials*   15

(c) *Applications*   16

    (i) Site damp-proof membranes   16
    (ii) Waterbars   19
    (iii) Damp-proof courses   22
    (iv) Tanking   22
    (v) Expansion joints   23
    (vi) Insulation (Thermal, acoustic, vibration)   24
    (vii) Pipes and Ducts   25
    (viii) Modifying properties of concrete by inclusion of plastics   .   26
    (ix) Bolt boxes and formers   26

SECTION FOUR: EXTERNAL WALLS, ROOFS, DOORS AND WINDOWS .   27

(a) *Introduction*   27
(b) *External Walls*   27

    (i) Profiled metal sheets with plastics coatings   27
    (ii) Composites of coated metal sheets and insulation   . . .   30
    (iii) Glass-reinforced plastics sheets (GRP sheets)   32
    (iv) Extruded unplasticised PVC sheets (UPVC sheeting) . . .   33
    (v) Acrylic sheets   35
    (vi) Infill panels to curtain walls   35
    (vii) Wall cladding units to framed buildings   35
    (viii) Cellular plastics   36
    (ix) Accessories   39

(c) *Sloping Roofs Incorporating Lap-Jointed Sheets*   39

    (i) Sloping roof constructions   40
    (ii) Roof slope (pitch) and sealing   40

(d) *Flat or Sloping Roofs Incorporating Continuous Waterproof*
    Layers   40

    (i) Components   40
    (ii) Structural decks   41
    (iii) Vapour barriers   41
    (iv) Insulation boards   41
    (v) Weather-proofing membranes   44
    (vi) Gutters   44

(e) *Accessories for Sloping and Flat Roofs*   45

    (i) Extruded unplasticised PVC and GRP verge trims   45
    (ii) Fascia gutters   45
    (iii) Glass-reinforced plastics flashings   45
    (iv) Pipe flashings   45
    (v) Roof outlets   45
    (vi) Screed ventilators   47

(f) *External and Internal Doors*   47

    (i) Characteristics of doors   47
    (ii) Flush doors   47
    (iii) Panelled doors   47
    (iv) Glazed doors   48
    (v) Flexible doors   48
    (vi) Sliding and lifting doors   49
    (vii) Door accessories   50

(g) *Windows*   51

    (i) Characteristics of windows   51
    (ii) Plastics glazing   52
    (iii) Plastics window frames   52
    (iv) Metal and wood frames with plastics covering   54
    (v) Gaskets and sealing strips   56
    (vi) Accessories   57

CONTENTS

SECTION FIVE: CEILINGS 58

   (a) *Definitions* 58

   (b) *Ceilings* (General) 58

   (c) *Ceiling Materials* (see also sub-section (e)) 58

   (d) *Suspended Ceilings* 59

   (e) *Materials for Suspended Ceilings* (see also sub-section (c)) . . . 61

SECTION SIX: PARTITIONS 63

   (a) *Introduction* 63

   (b) *Selection of Partitions – Factors Involved* 63

   (c) *Permanent Partitions* 64

      (i) Brick and block partitions 64
      (ii) Dry-construction partitions 65

   (d) *Demountable Partitions – Materials Used* 65

   (e) *Sliding and Folding Partitions* 66

SECTION SEVEN: FLOORING 67

   (a) *Introduction* 67

   (b) *Thermoplastic Tiles* 67

      (i) Tile sizes 68
      (ii) Methods of laying tiles 68
      (iii) Selection factors 68

   (c) *Vinyl Asbestos Tiles* 68

      (i) Tile sizes 69
      (ii) Method of laying tiles 69
      (iii) Selection factors 69

   (d) *Flexible Polyvinyl Chloride Tiles and Sheets* 69

      (i) Sizes 70
      (ii) Methods of laying 70
      (iii) Selection factors 70

   (e) *Other Methods of Using PVC in Flooring Materials* 71

      (i) Backing materials 71
      (ii) Flooring finishes 71
      (iii) PVC sheet 71
      (iv) Flexible vinyl sheet 71
      (v) Patterned vinyl 72

(f) *Carpeting*   72

(g) *Jointless Flooring*   72

     (i) Types of jointless flooring materials   72
    (ii) Applications   72

(h) *Floating Floor Quilts*   73

SECTION EIGHT: SERVICES   74

(a) *Introduction*   74

(b) *Water Mains and Services*   74

     (i) General   74
    (ii) Polyethylene water service pipe   74
   (iii) Unplasticised PVC water pipe   75
   (iv) Handling and storage   76

(c) *Gas Mains and Services*   76

     (i) General   76
    (ii) Fuel gases   76
   (iii) Distribution of non-fuel gases   77

(d) *Vacuum Lines*   77

     (i) General   77
    (ii) Materials and jointing   77

(e) *Instrument Lines*   77

     (i) Materials   77
    (ii) Jointing   78
   (iii) Advantages and disadvantages   78

(f) *Ventilation Equipment*   78

     (i) General   78
    (ii) Advantages of plastics for duct-work   80
   (iii) Materials available   80
   (iv) Working temperatures   83
    (v) Handling and fixing   83
   (vi) Handling and storage   85

(g) *Soil and Waste-Water Systems (above ground)*   85

     (i) General   85
    (ii) Soil pipes (Unplasticised PVC)   85
   (iii) Types of soil pipe systems   86
   (iv) Fixing soil pipes   86
    (v) Waste-pipe systems   88
   (vi) Types of waste-pipe systems   89
  (vii) Fixing of waste-pipe systems   89

(h) *Rainwater Systems* 89

    (i)   General 89
    (ii) Characteristics of unplasticised PVC rainwater systems . . 90
    (iii) Types of unplasticised PVC rainwater systems 90
    (iv) Fixing and accessories (see Fig. 8/7) 91
    (v)   Recommendations for safe fixing 92
    (vi) Flow rate 92
    (vii) Maintenance 92

(j) *Underground Drainage* 92

    (i)   General 92
    (ii) Handling and storage 93
    (iii) Installation and back-filling 93
    (iv) Inspection chambers 93
    (v)   Rodding 96
    (vi) Road gullies 96
    (vii) Economic considerations 96

(k) *Electrical Services* 96

    (i)   Cables 96
    (ii) Cable trays 98
    (iii) Conduit 98
    (iv) Skirting, architrave and trunking 99
    (v)   Luminaires (lighting fittings) and other fittings 100
    (vi) High-voltage and medium-voltage switchgear 100
    (vii) Earthing requirements 100

SECTION NINE: JOINTING AND SEALANTS 101

(a) *General (and Glossary)* 101

(b) *Definitions of Joints* 101

(c) *Selection of Sealants* 101

(d) *Application of Sealants* 103

    (i)   Surface preparation 103
    (ii) Application skill 104
    (iii) Climatic considerations 104
    (iv) Handling and storage 105

(e) *Flexible Sealants* 105

    (i)   Silicones 105
    (ii) Polysulphides 105
    (iii) Polyurethanes 106
    (iv) Acrylics 106
    (v)   Butyls 107
    (vi) Oil-based sealants 107
    (vii) Bituminous sealants 107
    (viii) Polyisobutylene (PIB) sealants (non-hardening) 108
    (ix) Preformed foam strips (non-hardening) 108

(f) *Rigid Sealants*   109

    (i) Epoxy resins   109
    (ii) Epoxy polysulphides   109

SECTION TEN: ADHESIVES   111

(a) *Introduction*   111

(b) *Types of Adhesives*   111

    (i) Non-reactive systems   111
    (ii) Reactive systems   111
    (iii) Combined systems   112

(c) *Nature of the Bond Obtained*   112

(d) *Recommended Practices When Using Plastics Adhesives* . . .   112

    (i) Manufacturer's instructions   112
    (ii) Surfaces to be bonded   112
    (iii) Applying the adhesive   113
    (iv) Handling two-part adhesives   113
    (v) Applying pressure   113
    (vi) Curing or maturing processes   113
    (vii) Effects of external conditions   114
    (viii) Hazards   114
    (ix) Storage   114

(e) *Adhesives for Specific Applications*   114

    (i) Floor coverings   114
    (ii) Wall coverings   115
    (iii) Bonding of other materials   115
    (iv) Bonding of structures   116

SECTION ELEVEN: ADDITIVES   117

(a) *Introduction*   117

(b) *Rubber Latex/Cement Compositions*   117

    (i) General   117
    (ii) Applications   118
    (iii) Properties   118

(c) *Synthetic Resin Latex/Cement Compositions*   118

    (i) General   118
    (ii) Applications   118
    (iii) Properties   119

(d) *Polyester Resin/Cement Compositions*   119

    (i) General   119
    (ii) Applications   120
    (iii) Properties   120

(e) *Economic Considerations*   121

SECTION TWELVE: BUILDING ACCESSORIES   122

  (a) *Introduction*   122

  (b) *Complete Units*   122

  (c) *Plastics Panels and Facings*   124

  (d) *Transparent and Translucent Materials*   125

  (e) *Sculptured Finishes*   126

  (f) *Sanitary Goods*   127

  (g) *Door and Window Fittings*   131

  (h) *Stairways*   132

  (j) *Signs and Letterings*   133

  (k) *Plastics-Coated Metal*   133

  (l) *Other Uses of Plastics in Building Accessories*   134

    (i) Neoprene and nylon   134
    (ii) Glass-reinforced plastics   134
    (iii) Plastics spraying   134
    (iv) Shutters, louvres, and blinds   137

SECTION THIRTEEN: TEMPORARY AIDS TO BUILDING   138

  (a) *Introduction*   138

  (b) *Weather Protection and Screening*   138

    (i) Materials   138
    (ii) Shelter units   139
    (iii) Precautions to be observed   140

  (c) *Pneumatic Buildings*   140

    (i) Advantages   140
    (ii) Operating requirements   141

  (d) *Buildings with Pneumatic Frames*   141

  (e) *Plastic Used to Protect Construction Materials*   141

  (f) *Temporary Pipework*   142

  (g) *Plastics and Formwork for Concrete*   142

    (i) Linings of polyethylene sheet   142
    (ii) Nylon coating for steel shutters   142
    (iii) Resin-impregnated plywood   142
    (iv) Glass-reinforced plastics forms   142
    (v) Polypropylene preformed moulds   143
    (vi) Surface finishes   143

  (h) *Curing Membranes*   144

    (i) Use of plastics sheets   144
    (ii) Liquid plastics spraying   144

(j) *Tools (and Accessories)*   145

(k) *Ropes*   145

     (i) Materials   145
     (ii) Properties   145
     (iii) Using plastics ropes   145

(l) *Forming Pockets in Concrete*   146

(m) *Protective Clothing*   146

APPENDIX A: CHARACTERISTICS OF PLASTICS USED IN BUILDING .   147

(a) *Introduction*   147

(b) *Thermoplastic Materials*   147

     1. Polyvinyl chloride (PVC)   147
     2. Polyethylene (PE)   148
     3. Polypropylene (PP)   149
     4. Polystyrene (PS)   150
     5. Acrylonitrile-butadiene-styrene (ABS)   151
     6. Polymethyl methacrylate (PMMA)   151

(c) *Thermosetting Materials*   151

     1. Phenolics and amino plastics   151
     2. Unsaturated polyesters   152
     3. Epoxy resins   152
     4. Polyurethanes (PUR)   153

APPENDIX B: BIBLIOGRAPHY AND SOME RELEVANT BRITISH
             STANDARDS   154

APPENDIX C: IMPERIAL/METRIC (SI) EQUIVALENTS   161

ACKNOWLEDGEMENTS   162

SECTION ONE

INTRODUCTION TO PLASTICS AND RUBBERS

(a) General Notes on Plastics

This section gives practical information on the use of plastics materials for those responsible for building design, construction or maintenance.

When considering the application of these materials for building purposes (e.g. for building components, cladding, protection, or decoration, etc.), account must be taken of relevant building regulations. In this Handbook, however, the applications described are not limited to those now allowed by current regulations since these are liable to modification.

The advantages of using plastics are first described, and general information then given on their use. The more important of the plastics used in buildings and their physical properties are for example dealt with in sub-section (d), and are followed by a short note on rubbers since these play a more modest role.

This information will also help those with little knowledge of plastics to appreciate their suitability for building purposes, and to consider building problems in terms of plastics and their successful application. It should be clearly understood, however, that design must be based on the characteristics of the plastics materials themselves — their use as a mere replacement for other (traditional) materials can often produce unsatisfactory results.

Other sections deal with economic factors and with various applications.

(b) Advantages of Plastics in Building

These advantages are summarised below, though it should be understood that not *all* are valid for *all* plastics. A judicious choice, however, will enable most of the required features or characteristics to be obtained by using one or more materials:—

(i)   Favourable strength to weight ratio of plastics building components. This facilitates handling, and consequently transport, storage and assembly.

(ii) Many variations may be obtained in shape, colour, surface pattern, either with standard or custom made items.

(iii) Little maintenance is required (see iv).

(iv) Plastics are ideal materials for the mass production of elements of improved and more consistent quality — sensitivity to seasonal influences plays no part in their manufacture. They are, therefore, particularly suitable for system building using prefabricated elements; this allows much of the building work to be transferred from site to factory and so results in faster and sometimes more economic production.

1

(v) Plastics-processing techniques are often simple, machine residence times are short, while the energy required per unit volume is low. Furthermore, highly-skilled labour is not often required.

(c) Factors Involved in the Use of Plastics

The extent to which a plastics material can be successfully used in building components depends on several factors such as dimensional stability, weathering and fire-resistant properties, thermal and acoustic properties etc., details of which are described below:—

(i) *Dimensional stability — stress rupture*

The dimensional stability of a material used for structural applications depends on its rigidity and thus on its elastic modulus and dimensions. This modulus is often determined from short-term tests. Plastics are less elastic than steel and other building materials; they are subject to "creep" and in consequence the deformation at a given load increases with time. This "creep" accelerates as the load increases, and the elastic modulus therefore falls as load and time increases.

In order to avoid excessive creep, a plastic material should first be tested at sustained loads over long periods so as to obtain results which enable creep deformation to be predicted. This in turn enables dimensions to be calculated for a plastic part which will not deform beyond a predetermined limit under a given load.

Another criterion may be the actual prevention of failure. The prediction of a safe service life is made on the basis of stress-rupture tests, though rupture itself also depends on time and stress. Because of the general lack of plastics design data, the British Standards Institution began publication of standard methods* for the determination and presentation of the information needed. Design data for plastics pipes is further advanced than that for other plastics components, and bursting times at various pressures (stresses) have been obtained which by extrapolation give life expectancies of up to 50 years.

Plastics have hitherto been applied mainly in non-load bearing or in lightly stressed constructions constituting parts of so called mixed buildings in which overall strength and rigidity are provided by steel and concrete etc. Their use for load-bearing functions in buildings of composite construction or even in "all plastics" buildings is comparatively rare, though such examples include the use of shell-shaped elements and of plastics space structures to constitute a roof. The low elastic modulus of plastics, however, necessitates the use of dimensionally large components in order to attain the required dimensional stability: this in turn involves higher costs.

(ii) *Colour fastness and weather resistance*

As with other materials, colour fastness may also be significant. For indoor applications, correct pigmentation can ensure that plastics of various colours

---

* B.S. 4618 Recommendations for the Presentation of Plastics Design Data (Parts 1 to 5 as at 1972).

may be used and remain unchanged. In outdoor use, however, colour fastness depends generally on the influence of the weather.

The ageing of plastics due to weathering is a complicated process – for example, temperature and humidity changes result in moisture absorption or evaporation, while ultra-violet rays (sunshine) may also affect them. The study of their weather resistance properties is also difficult since there has been so far little correlation between results from laboratory tests on the exposure of plastics to moisture and radiation and those obtained from natural weathering. In some cases, stabilisers and/or pigments are incorporated to ensure the required weather resistance. The selection of these is important since the success or durability of a weather-resistant plastic depends largely on proper pigmentation.

Weather resistance must always be seriously considered when selecting plastics components for building purposes. Slight deviations from a proven standard of pigmentation system has necessitated the painting of plastics panels after a period of service, whereas those with the standard pigmentation have remained satisfactory. The effect of weathering, however, is often limited to small surface layers, and the mechanical properties of a weathered sheet may not deteriorate.

(iii) *Safety from fire*

Fire risks are always an important factor in any building, and must be taken into account when plastics are to be used as construction materials, Flammability itself need not militate against the use of plastics materials, most of which are flammable to some degree (as are some other building materials such as wood). The extent to which they can be safely used from a fire risk standpoint must be carefully considered however.

There are large differences between the flammability of the various plastics. Some, such as polyethylene burn readily when once ignited; others, like PVC are self-extinguishing in that they burn only while fed by a flame and extinguish themselves when the flame is removed. All such differences must be taken into account. If necessary, reasonable safety requirements can often be met by mixing in "fire-retardant" materials or by chemically incorporating certain others. Examples include self-extinguishing polystyrene foam and self-extinguishing polyester and epoxide resins.

It should be remembered that although the addition of properly selected fire-resistant materials may provide permanent resistance, some gradually lose their fire retardent properties through ageing or by long exposure to temperatures above normal ambient, or due to humidity. There are, nevertheless, conditions under which "flammable" plastics may be allowed provided that they are used in combination with non-flammable materials.

Like some woods, plastics materials if involved in a fire may exude heavy smoke and fumes that may be toxic and their use in stairways and corridors should be carefully considered, since escape from a building should not be hampered. The observance of existing regulations helps to reduce fire hazards in completed buildings incorporating plastics components, but during construction, plastics may often be stored or used in various concentrations without regard to the safety aspects applicable to a completed building. Steps should therefore be taken to minimise any dangers or difficulties likely to arise from accidental "plastic" fires, e.g. from the release of HCl gas from burning PVC. Furthermore waste plastics products should not be disposed of by being burnt on construction sites.

The proportion and nature of plastics materials (and their location) should always be taken into account when assessing fire risks and consequential dangers.

(iv) *Resistance to water and water vapour*

Most plastics have low water absorption properties and low water vapour permeability, and are superior to other building materials in these respects. They are therefore particularly suitable as impervious membranes in foundations to prevent ingress of ground water, as protective films for building materials stored on site, and for use in sanitary installations. Any water absorption produces no perceptible change in the dimensions of a plastic material or component.

(v) *Thermal expansion*

The coefficient of thermal expansion of plastics materials is usually higher than that of other building materials and should be taken into account. The variations in length of PVC guttering due to temperature changes are for example taken up by flexible joints, while slotted bolt holes have been used in plastics sheeting to allow for thermal expansion or contraction.

The expansion of materials with high thermal coefficients may be restricted when they form part of a composite material – that of glass-reinforced resin for instance is lower than that of thermoplastics in general, since intermediate values are obtained from laminates of two different materials.

(vi) *Thermal insulation*

The thermal insulation of sandwich constructions filled for example, with polyurethane foam or expanded polystyrene is much greater than that of walls built-up from conventional materials; thus 25-mm thick polyurethane foam provides as much thermal insulation as 500-mm brick: other foams also have similar insulating properties.

(vii) *Acoustic insulation*

A high value of mass per unit of surface area is needed in order to provide good acoustic insulation. Such insulation may therefore be poor with plastics used for thermal insulating purposes. Thus improved thermal insulation gained by using plastics foam or expanded plastics as a core in a partition wall can be offset by a loss in air-borne sound insulation. This loss can however be reduced or compensated by using for example either a double-wall construction with a flexible plastics film hanging loose in the cavity, or a double wall with cores built up of various layers. The acoustic insulation of panels or walls will be improved by keeping the rigidity of the layers as low as possible — a requirement contrary to that needed from the structural stand-point. An "ideal" lightweight partition wall will of necessity be a compromise between these requirements.

Impact sound insulation is generally less important for partition walls than for floor and ceiling constructions — in these the use of plastics foams usually has a favourable effect (increasing the insulation), as for example when expanded polystyrene is employed as an elastic underlay for floating floors.

(d) The More Important Plastics in Building (and Physical Properties)

(i) *Types of plastics used*

The large variety of plastics materials that have been used for building applications is indicated in Table 1/1. To avoid being confused by this variety, it is advisable to classify the plastics into two main groups, namely the *thermoplastics* and *thermosetting* materials, and for convenience the more important plastics are grouped under these headings in Table 1/2.

Thermoplastics soften and melt gradually when heated and can be shaped or reshaped when warm. Thermosetting materials, however, cannot be reshaped after manufacture since their constituent molecules are bonded in all directions, so that heat (within limits) cannot effect molecular structure.

(ii) *Physical properties*

Only selected properties are referred to here, since the plastics industry has been blamed, not without some reason, for readiness to present long impressive lists of properties that have little practical value. Table 1/3, therefore, indicates certain physical properties of some important thermoplastics and thermo-setting materials. The strength properties are useful for comparison purposes, but from the standpoint of the building industry, only the permissible design stresses are of value.

Table 1/4 compares the engineering properties of conventional building materials (steel and concrete) with those of typical thermoplastics and thermosetting materials used for building applications (PVC, and glass-reinforced plastics). Glass-reinforced plastics can be made from a number of resins, but the properties of the glass as well as the percentage used for rein-forcement may vary, and the permissible tensile stress is therefore given as a range.

Column 3 of Table 1/4 indicates that the "short-term" tensile strength of thermoplastics (PVC) is less than that of glass-reinforced polyesters, whose strength in the stronger ranges would seem quite satisfactory. These "short-term" values, however, are obtained from tests of short duration, (a few minutes) and lower values are given by tensile tests of long duration. This "time-effect" is less marked with other materials like steel and concrete. Col. 4 indicates permissible design stresses which take this "time-effect" into account.

In the present state of knowledge, only indicative values can be given for safe design stresses of plastics materials. In tank construction for example a safety factor of about 10.0 is often adopted for glass-reinforced polyester, whereas for thermoplastics (e.g. PVC) only the permissible stress for extruded

TABLE 1/1: PLASTICS AND RUBBERS USED IN THE BUILDING INDUSTRY

(1)	(2) Resins — Thermosetting materials							(3) Thermoplastic materials												(4) Rubbers — General-purpose			(4) Rubbers — Special-purpose				
Applications	Phenolic resin (PF)	Urea resin (UF)	Melamine resin (MF)	Unsaturated polyesters (UP)	Epoxies (EP)	Polyurethanes (PUR)	Silicones (SI)	Polyvinylchloride, unplasticised (PVC)	Polyvinylchloride, plasticised (PVC)	Polyvinyl acetate (PVAC)	Polystyrene (PS)	Polyethylene (PE)	Polypropylene (PP)	Polyisobutylene (PIB)	Acrylonitrile-butadiene-styrene (ABS)	Acrylics	Polyamides (e.g. Nylons) (PA)	Cumarone-indene resin	Cellulose acetate (CA)	Natural & synthetic isoprene rubber	Styrene butadiene rubber	Polybutadiene rubber	Ethylene propylene rubber	Butyl rubber	Polychloroprene	Nitrile rubber	Polysulphide rubber
CONCRETE STRUCTURES																											
Moulds				X	X																		X	X	X		
Shuttering for columns								X																			
Shuttering for sections				X	X																						
Lining for shuttering	X							X	X		X	X	X										X	X	X		
Reinforcing bar spacers												X															
Cement mortar for repairs					X					X																	
Membranes chem. resistant									X			X		X									X	X	X	X	X
Seals for expansion joints						X			X					X									X				X
Foam blocks for pocket holes											X																

	1	2	3	4	5	6	7	8	9	10	11
WALLS											
Sandwich type panels: core	X						X				
Sandwich type panels: facing	X	X	X				X	X			
Hollow type panels	X						X				
Sheets, flat and profiled	X	X					X		X		
Sheets, transparent		X					X	X			
Gaskets (structural)							X	X			X X X X X / X X X
DOORS											
Folding doors, flap doors							X			X	
Rolling grilles, dipcoated							X		X	X	
Sandwich type doors, facing	X	X					X				
Sandwich type doors, core			X				X	X			
Swing door, transparent							X		X		
Sliding gear										X	
WINDOWS											
Cold Bridge								X		X	X
Glazing sheets and foils		X					X		X		
Glazing beads							X	X			
Weather strips							X	X		X	X
Condensation sections							X				
Sections with metal or wooden core							X		X	X	
Sections all plastics			X				X	X			
Jointing and caulking material							X	X	X	X	X
Sun protection							X	X			
Sealants and gaskets							X	X	X	X	X
FLOORS											
Foam sheets for floating floors							X				

TABLE 1/1: PLASTICS AND RUBBERS USED IN THE BUILDING INDUSTRY (contd.)

Applications	(2) Resins — Thermosetting materials							(3) Thermoplastic materials												(4) Rubbers — General-purpose			Special-purpose				
	Phenolic resin (PF)	Urea resin (UF)	Melamine resin (MF)	Unsaturated polyesters (UP)	Epoxies (EP)	Polyurethanes (PUR)	Silicones (SI)	Polyvinylchloride, unplasticised (PVC)	Polyvinylchloride, plasticised (PVC)	Polyvinyl Acetate (PVAC)	Polystyrene (PS)	Polyethylene (PE)	Polypropylene (PP)	Polyisobutylene (PIB)	Acrylonitrile-butadiene-styrene (ABS)	Acrylics	Polyamides (e.g. Nylons) (PA)	Cumarone-indene resin	Cellulose acetate (CA)	Natural & synthetic isoprene rubber	Styrene butadiene rubber	Polybutadiene rubber	Ethylene propylene rubber	Butyl rubber	Polychloroprene	Nitrile rubber	Polysulphide rubber
ROOFS																											
Vapour barriers												X															
Roof lights and domes				X												X											
Corrugated and flat sheets				X				X								X											
INSULATION																											
Expanded beads as concrete filler											X																
Foam sheets	X	X				X		X			X																
Foam applied in situ.		X				X																					
SANITATION, DRAINAGE AND UTILITIES																											
Cisterns, flush pipes and floats								X				X	X		X				X								
Disposal systems								X				X	X														
Pipes, fittings, fixtures and taps								X				X	X		X				X								
Rain gutters				X				X				X															
Baths				X												X											

Toilet and urinal bowls				X												X											
Traps, floor drains and syphons								X				X	X														
Electrical switches, junction boxes	X		X					X																			
Electrical conduit								X																			
Airducts				X				X					X														
Ventilators and grilles								X					X				X										
Flexible joints and seals for pipes & taps												X								X	X						
FINISHING																											
Ceiling – tiles sheet						X					X																
Floor – sheets									X											X	X	X	X				
Floor – tiles									X									X		X	X	X	X				
Floor – jointless				X	X					X																	
Walls – panel facings	X		X	X				X																			
Walls – Veneers	X		X																								
Walls – Tiles and sheets								X			X																
Walls – Wall cloth									X																		
Walls – Waterproofing and pore filling material							X			X																	
Roof sheeting									X														X	X			
Stair nosing								X	X											X	X	X	X				
MISCELLANEOUS																											
Covers (temporary weather protection)									X			X											X	X	X		
Adhesives	X	X	X		X	X				X				X						X	X			X	X	X	X
Fencing dipcoated									X																		
Shrink covers (handrails)									X																		
Ropes												X	X				X										
Hardware and ironmongery	X	X	X					X					X				X										
Flag poles				X	X																						
Hoses									X											X	X	X	X	X	X	X	
Cables insulation/sheathing									X			X								X	X	X	X	X	X		X

TABLE 1/2: MAIN PLASTICS MATERIALS USED IN BUILDING –
COVERING MOST APPLICATIONS

(for properties, see Appendix A)

Thermoplastics (with symbol)		Thermosetting materials (with symbol)	
Polyvinyl chloride	PVC*	Unsaturated polyesters (+)	UP
Polyethylene	PE	Epoxides+	EP
Polypropylene	PP	Phenolformaldehyde	PF
Polystyrene	PS	Polyurethane	PUR
Polymethylmethacrylate	PMMA		

* Plasticised PVC (to which plasticisers have been added) is more flexible. High impact PVC
contains additives to increase impact resistance.

+ Unsaturated polyesters and epoxy resins when used in association with glass reinforcement
are referred to as GRP (See Appendix A).

pipe can be given. The value of 11 to 12 MN/m^2 cited for PVC in Col. 4 is
higher than those generally accepted for the safe design stresses of other
important thermoplastics such as low density polyethylene (3.2 MN/m^2), high-
density polyethylene (5 MN/m^2), polypropylene (5 MN/m^2) – all such values
are for room temperatures.

The elastic moduli values given in Col. 5 of Table 1/4 show that the stiffness of plastics, even of glass-reinforced resin, is much lower than that of steel
– this being one reason why plastics are not generally used for load bearing
purposes in building, i.e. their lower strength and stiffness tend to outweigh
their advantage of low density (Col. 2).

(e) General Note on Rubbers Used in Building

Rubbers play a less important role in building than either thermoplastics or
thermosetting materials. They are mainly used as membranes, sealants or gaskets,
where flexibility and impermeability to water moisture are required. The good
weather-resistance properties of properly selected rubbers are specially useful for
roofing applications, cables and hoses etc., and their abrasion resistance is fully
utilised in flooring materials.

Table 1/1 also indicates the applications of the rubbers used in building; butyl
rubber and polychloroprene (neoprene) are often employed.

TABLE 1/3: PHYSICAL PROPERTIES OF PLASTICS MOST COMMONLY USED

("Indicative" values at normal room temperature)

(1) Material	(2) Density kg/m^3	(3) Tensile strength MN/m^2	(4) Compressive strength MN/m^2	(5) Modulus of elasticity GN/m^2	(6) Coefficient of thermal expansion $°C^{-1}$ $(\times 10^{-6})$	(7) Thermal conductivity (k) $W/m \ °C$
Polyvinyl chloride (PVC)	1400	52.5	63	2.80	50	0.25
Polyethylene						
Low-density	915 to 930	12.5	–	0.175	280	0.29
High-density	935 to 960	24.0	21	0.770	130	0.40
Polypropylene	900 to 910	35.0	42	1.19	120	0.23
Filled phenol formaldehyde	1600 to 1750	10 to 28	70 to 100	6.30	25	0.35
Glass-reinforced epoxy*	1500 to 1700*	70 to 180*	–	5.0 to 13.0*	18 to 32*	0.20 to 0.28*
Glass-reinforced polyester*	1500 to 1700*	70 to 180*	–	5.0 to 13.0*	18 to 32*	0.20 to 0.28*

* With 30 to 50 per cent by weight of chopped strand mat. Long-term tests indicate that glass-reinforced epoxy resin has a higher fatigue strength than glass-reinforced polyester resin.

TABLE 1/4: COMPARISON OF SOME "ENGINEERING" PROPERTIES

(Typical plastics, steel, and concrete as building materials)

(1)	(2)	(3)	(4)	(5)	(6)
	Density	*Tensile strength MN/m²*		*Modulus of elasticity*	*Coefficient of thermal expansion*
Material	*kg/m³*	*Short term*	*Permissible design stress*	*GN/m²*	*°C⁻¹*
					$(\times 10^{-6})$
Polyvinyl chloride (PVC)	1400	50	11 to 12	3.0	50
Glass-reinforced polyester*	1500 to 2000*	70 to 400*	7 to 50*	5 to 25*	18 to 32*
Mild steel	7800	–	150	200	12
Concrete (1:2:4 mixes)**	2500	–	7 (in compression)	14	7 to 12

* Values given depend on type of reinforcement, cf. Table 1/3.

** Concrete is normally used under compression.

ECONOMIC CONSIDERATIONS

It is sometimes difficult to appraise the economics of using plastics in building. The comparitively high cost of the raw material is offset by inexpensive mass production processes to give finished plastics products, which are often cheaper to use than traditional building materials or components.

Direct cost comparisons can be made where a plastic article can be employed instead of one in another material, e.g. as for rain-water pipes and gutters. More usually, however, other factors are also involved e.g. translucent roof sheeting cannot be directly compared with patent glazing without also taking into account the cost of associated steel rails, flashings, ease of handling as well as the speed of fixing.

In making cost comparisons between plastics and other materials, the inherent advantages and disadvantages of the materials themselves must also be taken into account. Even though these cannot always be actually costed, the following factors should be considered:—

1. *Cost of individual articles*

There is no basis for assessing the economic advantage of using plastics when they cannot be directly compared with other materials, as in the case of some plastics adhesives and jointing compounds. It may be possible to take into account the actions necessary in the absence of plastics, but this would compare unlike procedures and so fail to give a fair appraisal.

The costs of similar articles made in more than one plastics material (e.g. baths from acrylics or made from glass-reinforced plastics) may also be sufficiently similar as to show no marked advantage for the plastics. In such cases, selection must depend largely on appearance and performance (durability) — see (3) below.

2. *Maintenance costs*

The apparent saving in maintenance costs offered by the use of certain materials needs careful consideration. For example, plastics usually have a good surface finish and may appear to require little or no maintenance. Some however tend to attract dirt because of their electrostatic properties and ability to hold electric charges. Such plastics may in time require painting, and the claim that they are "self-finished" and reduce maintenance cannot always be justified.

This claim can sometimes be supported, however, and should be offset against initial costs whenever it can.

3. *Initial marketing costs*

Values are constantly changing. Articles that seem expensive when first marketed become cheaper when well established. At the same time goods which are likely to be displaced by them are forced to become more competitive; there must, therefore, be a period of market adjustment.

As indicated in 1 to 3 above, it is difficult to present reliable data on the costs of plastics materials. Any guidance on this subject could prove misleading especially if it failed to take full account of other relevant considerations for a particular building.

Throughout this Handbook, therefore, there is little reference to economic factors though some indications of relative costs are given wherever possible.

SECTION THREE

FOUNDATIONS

(a) Introduction

One of the main problems in foundation work is the movement of moisture, either by permeation through concrete slabs and joints during the life of a building or by being trapped within slabs following the long drying out periods required for thick slabs.

Plastics materials are being used for various applications in foundation work. Owing to their high resistance to moisture penetration, their rot-proof qualities, and their long life stability they are giving better performance than many conventional materials. They are also easily handled and positioned, and this combined with the advantages just mentioned can bring about useful economies, especially as they can be readily shaped and extruded into convenient sections and so be used for a variety of purposes.

Polyethylene, PVC, and butyl rubber are available as films and sheets in a range of thicknesses; they can also be extruded into a number of forms such as tubes, ducts, water bars etc. Polyester and glass fibre can be "laid up" manually in moulds to produce the finally required form; they can also be formed in press-operated moulds.

Cellular plastics are available as sheets, boards and blocks in sizes at present up to 3.6 m by 1.2 m. They can be laminated to other products (e.g. paper, plywood, metal) to produce composite materials. Some of the cellular plastics can also be extruded or shaped into pipe insulation sections etc.

(b) Plastics Materials

The plastics listed on Table 3/1 are used in foundation work for the purposes indicated.

TABLE 3/1: PLASTICS MATERIALS ASSOCIATED WITH FOUNDATION WORK

(1)	(2)
Material	*Form or Purpose*
Polyethylene Plasticised PVC Butyl rubber.	Flexible sheets and extruded sections.
Expanded rubber Expanded polyethylene	Flexible cellular material.
Expanded polystyrene Expanded ebonite Polyurethane foam	Rigid cellular boards.
Polyester glass fibre	Rigid sheets.

Much experience has been gained on the resistance of these plastics (Table 3/1) to the materials or agents likely to be met in foundation work. They are for example generally resistant to water, acids, alkalis and fungi, though PVC can be softened by some types of oil. The cellular plastics, however, are too permeable for use as damp-proof membranes.

Plastics materials are flexible enough to take up, without fracture, any slight movement in a structure that may result (at other than purpose made movement joints) from shrinkage, settlement or thermal expansion or contraction, etc. They are poor heat and sound conductors especially the expanded plastics, and can be successfully used under and around the edges of floor screeds and beneath partition walls etc. to reduce the transmission of heat and sound.

(c) Applications

The main applications of plastics in foundation work are discussed below in items (i) to (ix) and cover:-

> Site damp-proof membranes.
> Waterbars.
> Damp-proof courses.
> Tanking.
> Expansion joints.
> Insulation.
> Pipes and ducts.
> Modifying properties of concrete (by inclusion of plastics).
> Bolt boxes and formers.

(i) *Site damp-proof membranes*

The plastics used for this purpose are:—
> Polyethylene (which should comply with B.S. 3012).
> Plasticised PVC (with PVC conforming to B.S. 1763).
> Butyl rubber.
> Polyisobutylene sheet.
> Glass reinforced epoxy coal tar mixtures.

Problems created by damp rising through concrete floors, such as damp surfaces, transport of ground salts, damage to floor finish, can be minimised or prevented by the use of an overall damp-proof membrane. Such membranes are normally only required to resist the movement of water by capillary action and not that resulting from hydrostatic heads.

The degree of damp-proofing required, its durability, construction and resistance to damage, as well as ground and water table conditions must all be considered in selecting the type and thickness of membrane (sheeting) and the joint sealing methods for a particular project. Resistance to the passage of moisture (good impermeability) is essential for example with a high ground water table and when a floor finish is susceptible to moisture from underneath. On the other hand a lower resistance would be acceptable where a self-finished concrete floor to a well ventilated shed is laid on well drained ground.

Damp-proof plastics membranes, as well as forming barriers to the upward

movement of moisture, can also serve as an underlay to concrete. They
prevent loss of fines and cement from newly placed concrete slabs in the
same way as building paper underlays; they can also serve as slip membranes.

Some plastics sheet materials are tougher and more resistant to penetration
than others. Possible damage to plastics sheets, however, depends largely on
the severity of the "traffic", the thickness and type of sheet, as well as on the
condition of the surfaces on which the sheets are laid. Small punctures can
possibly be tolerated when sheets are used as underlays to prevent loss of
grout, but could prove serious where impermeability to moisture is a first
requirement. The risk of sheets being damaged is reduced by using an under-
lying sand bed or layer of pulverised fuel ash. Typical methods of using sheets

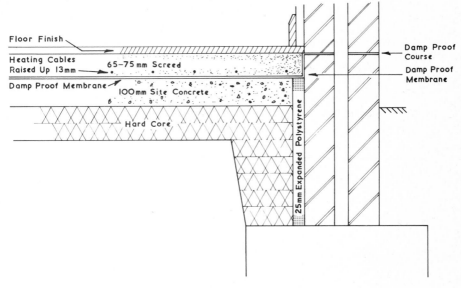

Fig. 3/1 Simple method of insulating a ground floor slab, using expanded polystyrene, –
showing also plastics sheeting as a damp-proof membrane.

in these applications are shown in Figs. 3/1, 3/2 and 3/3, relating to the
insulation of a ground floor slab.

As already indicated, the method of jointing plastics sheeting at the edges,
and also to damp-proof courses in walls depends upon the degree of damp-
proofing required. Lapping or folding at the joints will suffice in some
applications where a 100 per cent seal is unnecessary. In others, the joints
may have to be sealed by the use of adhesives, by heat welding or by other
methods (suitable for the type of sheeting) in order to provide the required
standard of imperviousness to moisture.

Polyethylene sheet can normally be obtained in thicknesses from 100 to
1500-gauge (0.025 mm to 0.381 mm approximately) and in widths up to about
7 m. 500-gauge is the minimum that should be used for most membrane
applications in foundation work, but 1000-gauge is recommended if it is
essential for the sheets to remain undamaged when the risk of damage during
construction is high. The practice of using two layers of 200-gauge sheets

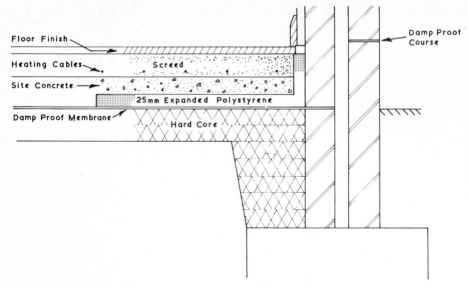

Fig. 3/2 Improved method of insulating a ground-floor slab, using expanded polystyrene –
         showing also plastics sheeting as a damp-proof membrane.

with staggered joints has not proved satisfactory, especially under arduous
site conditions, and is not recommended.

Folded joints at the edges are usually adequate for the duties required from
polyethylene sheets, with lapped joints at the junction of the membrane and
wall damp-proof course. A completely waterproof seal (between membrane

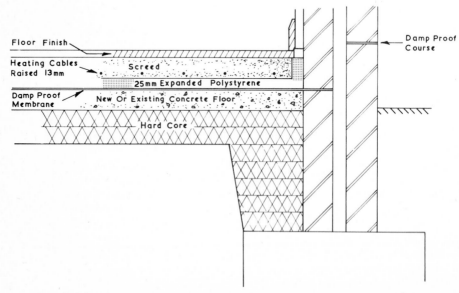

Fig. 3/3 Full insulation of a ground-floor slab, using expanded polystyrene – showing
         also plastics sheeting as a damp-proof membrane.

and damp-proof course) can be obtained when a polyethylene damp-proof course is used with a polyethylene sheet membrane. If however, PVC or butyl rubber sheet is to be used with a polyethylene damp-proof course, then lapping of the different materials provides the only satisfactory jointing method.

The main cause of degradation (i.e. sunlight) is prevented when polyethylene is used between or under concrete slabs, and the material should last indefinitely. Black pigmented grades however, offer greater resistance to the effects of sunlight.

Plasticised PVC is similar in many respects to polyethylene; it can be jointed by heat welding, or by folding and lapping, but cannot be jointed to polyethylene, other than by lapping; it is however generally slightly more permeable than polyethylene.

Butyl rubber is several times more expensive than polyethylene or plasticised PVC, but is more resistant to possible damage. If correctly compounded it has low permeability, similar to that of polyethylene. Its use is generally restricted to the tanking applications referred to in sub-section (iv) but the properties just mentioned may sometimes justify its selection for damp-proof membranes of the types just described. The material can be obtained in thicknesses from 0.5 mm to 1.5 mm for practical applications and in widths usually of 1.5 m, although it can be fabricated to any width in the factory. The preferred method of jointing is by a factory vulcanising process, though joints can be made on site by using self-adhesive strips.

Polyisobutylene is a similar material to butyl rubber, but cannot be vulcanised; at present it is more widely used in Europe than in the United Kingdom for building purposes.

Epoxy coal tar coatings can have glass fibre reinforcement. They are applied in liquid form, usually to rigid surfaces such as concrete. They can be used for example to line trenches etc. where surface variations would involve much cutting and jointing of sheet material.

The sizes of rolls or of sheet material used, depends largely on the handling facilities available, and polyethylene for example can be obtained to special order in widths greater than the 7 m previously mentioned.

(ii) *Waterbars*

Plasticised PVC waterbars, produced usually by extrusion, can be obtained for use in joints between concrete sections.

Joints between concrete beams or slabs, e.g. expansion joints, are often required to remain watertight when movement occurs, and the arrangement of the reinforcement adjacent to such joints enables this to take place without fracturing the concrete. Other forms of joint however, e.g. construction joints, are made or located when there is a break (stoppage) in concreting operations — in these instances, the continuity of the reinforcement prevents any movement in the joints.

PVC waterbars of the correct type and design for the joints involved can provide an effective seal against water pressures up to 450 kN/m^2 head. Lateral movements up to 12-mm, and even larger shear movements can be accommodated in expansion joints without failure of the waterbar. It is

essential however to use one of the correct section, and to seek the manufacturers' advice when necessary.

Figure 3/4 indicates a flat dumb bell section which is generally best suited
for construction joints. The dumb bell section with centre bulb depicted in
Fig. 3/5 gives the best results in expansion joints; the centre bulb enables

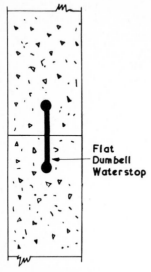

Flat
Dumbell
Waterstop

Fig. 3/4 Construction joint with
flat dumbell waterstop.

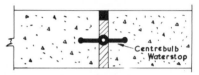

Centrebulb
Waterstop

Fig. 3/5 Expansion joint with centre-bulb
waterstop.

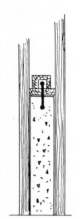

Fig. 3/6 Formwork used to hold waterstop
in position during casting of concrete.

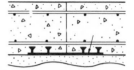

Fig. 3/7 Waterbar, developed to minimise
distortion, in a construction joint.

movement to occur without unduly straining the PVC. These waterbars can
be used in either horizontal or vertical joints — the usual method being to
cast one side of the waterbar in the first pour of concrete, while being held
in position as shown in Fig. 3/6. When the formwork is struck, the exposed
part of the waterbar is cleaned and concrete poured into the adjacent member
or slab.

It is essential to prevent distortion of the waterbar before and during concreting; to some extent this can be ensured by the use of clips, attached to the dumb-bell and wired to the reinforcement. A special type of waterbar developed to minimise distortion is indicated in Figs. 3/7 and 3/8, the waterbar being secured to the formwork before the concrete is placed.

Jointing of PVC waterbars is usually necessary, and has often to be carried out on site. The butt joint is the one which can be made most easily and satisfactorily on site; for this reason most manufacturers of PVC waterbars supply the more complicated intersections in ready made form, butt joints

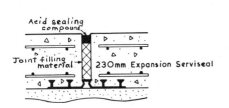

Fig. 3/8 Waterbar, developed to minimise distortion, in an expansion joint.

Fig. 3/9 Typical junction pieces for PVC waterbars.

being used to join these to a long length of waterstop. Some typical junction pieces are shown in Fig. 3/9.

One method of making a butt joint in a PVC waterbar is to cut the ends square, melt the PVC on the ends and butt them together while the material is still molten; the joint is then allowed to cool, excess PVC being trimmed off with a sharp knife. A simple jig, depicted in Fig. 3/10, can be used to

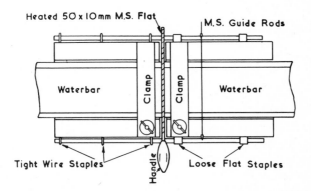

Fig. 3/10 Simple jig for holding waterbar in position during butt jointing.

clamp the waterbar in alignment and a heated plate in position during jointing. Fig. 3/11 shows the jig with the clamp in an open position. A bar of mild steel heated by a gas flame can be used for melting the PVC, though an electrically-heated plate usually gives the best results. A poor joint will be obtained if the heating plate is either too cool or too hot; in the former case the PVC will not be sufficiently heated, whereas overheating will cause charring and so produce a dry joint.

PVC has certain limitations as compared with rubber (which is also used
for waterbars) since the latter is more flexible and can therefore accommodate greater movements than those for which a PVC waterbar is suitable.
PVC jointing techniques however enable quicker and simpler joints to be
made, especially in bad weather, and PVC itself can resist certain con-
taminated ground conditions more effectively than rubber.

The only significant problems likely with plastic waterbars may arise when
they are incorporated into bunds around oil tanks. Highly-plasticised PVC

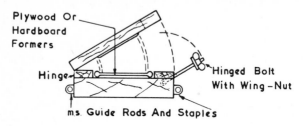

Plywood Or
Hardboard
Formers

Hinge

Hinged Bolt
With Wing-Nut

m.s. Guide Rods And Staples

Fig. 3/11 As for 3/10, but with clamp in "open" position.

for example can be affected by contact with oil, (resulting say from tank
leakage). If such bunds are to be used around tanks containing other organic
liquids, then the waterbar manufacturer should be consulted regarding
resistance to attack by the liquid involved. Such problems are unlikely to
arise however if the design of the joints in the concrete and the amount of
leakage prevent oil from coming into direct contact with the waterbar.

(iii) *Damp-proof courses*

Thick polyethylene and plasticised PVC sheeting are produced in long-
length rolls in normal widths for use as damp proof course materials in walls
built from bricks, blocks, etc. The same considerations apply to the position
of plastics damp-proof course in walls (whether solid or cavity) as apply to
conventional rigid or flexible materials. The plastics materials however have
the advantages of high strength, greater flexibility and ease of bending.

Polyethylene damp-proof courses have slight sliding properties (see B.S. 743:
Materials for Damp Proof Courses); these are not considered significant in
normal applications, but damp-proof courses from this material should not be
used in structures where the risk of sliding at damp-course level may constitute a hazard. B.S. 743 deals with the thicknesses, qualities and other properties of polyethylene damp-proof courses and includes useful notes on
their use.

(iv) *Tanking*

When selecting a material for damp-proofing a basement, consideration
must be given to the structure, water table and water pressure, type of
ground, method of construction and the use of the basement. In certain instances,
good impermeability is essential, whereas in others, slight leakage and passage
of moisture is of little consequence.

Most of the plastics and rubber sheet materials referred to in (i) of this
Section are suitable as water-resisting membranes in tanking applications, but
the selection of the material for a particular project depends on the characteristics required and on economic considerations.

Construction of basements waterproofed by plastics and rubber sheet
materials can proceed in weather conditions that would not permit asphalt
work to be carried out, since the comparatively dry surfaces required for the
application of asphalt are unnecessary. Polyethylene and plasticised PVC
sheeting can be used, though care must be taken to prevent the sheets being
damaged whilst being built in.

In a typical procedure for the construction of waterproof basement, the
floor slab is cast first. This is then covered with the plastics sheeting using
the lap and fold or the welted methods to make joints in the sheets. The
edges of the sheets are then turned, and again lapped and folded or welted to
the vertical sheets forming the sides of the tanking. These sheets are attached
to the shuttering forming the outer surface of the inner concrete wall. (Tack-
ing is an accepted method of attachment, but it punctures the sheets and this
can be a disadvantage; a cheap press-stud type of fixing is now available which
parts when the shuttering is struck thereby freeing the sheets without
puncturing them). The inner shuttering is erected and the concrete walls cast.
The outer shuttering is re-positioned, (leaving the plastics sheets attached to
the inner wall) to permit the casting of the outer wall. Concrete to the outer
wall is then poured, the sheeting being left embedded between the outer and
inner. A loading slab of concrete is laid over the sheeting on the structural
slab to form the floor of the basement.

The cost of repairing leaks in waterproofing membranes of tanked basements after construction, can be very high, and, in order to eliminate site
joints it is sometimes better to fabricate the whole of the membrane as a
single unit at the factory. It can then be transported to the site, placed inside
the basement and temporarily supported. The loading slab is cast and the
inner walls constructed. Ducts and apertures in the perimeter walls and floor
slab can be accommodated if precautions are taken to flash and seal the
membrane around pipe openings or other apertures.

The size of basement that can be waterproofed in this way depends upon
the handling facilities available for the complete membrane — basements up
to 18-metre square have been successfully constructed. Plasticised PVC and
butyl rubber have been used for fabricated membranes; butyl rubber is
particularly suited to the larger applications because of its good tear resistance and damp-proof qualities.

(v) *Expansion joints*

Expanded rigid cellular plastics boards can be used with or without waterbars to provide a gap between the concrete surfaces of an expansion joint. In
strip or sheet form they are positioned after the formwork is removed,
following the casting of the first member and before the pouring of the
adjacent concrete. Expanded rubber can also be used, especially for accom-
modating large joint movements. If the surface of the concrete in which the
joint is located is subject to traffic, then the upper surface of the jointing

material should be set below the wearing surface and the gap filled with a polysulphide or other suitable sealing compound.

Plasticised PVC in sheet or strip form is tough and resilient, and in suitable thicknesses is often used as a joint filling material. It is however, more suitable for joints that have to accommodate flexing of the structure, than for those that must accommodate temperature variation movements parallel to the axis of the slab or member.

(vi) *Insulation – (Thermal, acoustic and vibration)*

1. *Thermal insulation*

Cellular plastics like polystyrene, polyurethane and rigid vulcanised rubber are lightweight thermal insulating materials with very low heat conducting properties. Polystyrene board can now be obtained to comply with B.S. 3837 (Expanded Polystyrene Board for Thermal Insulation Properties).

The Board densities normally used for thermal insulation purposes are 16–40 kg/m^3 for polystyrene, 32 kg/m^3 for polyurethane, and 64 kg/m^3 for ebonite. The boards themselves can be laid as thermal barriers over the site concrete when electric underfloor heating is installed, and are usually covered by a protective layer of sand-cement screed before the heating cables are laid.

Provided that the correct grade is selected these materials are not unduly compressed by floor loads arising during the use of a building – furthermore they do not absorb moisture or cement fines from finishing screeds, and so, for both of these reasons retain their full insulating properties from the time of installation. Manufacturers should be consulted however over the selection of the type of insulating board for a particular loading. A waterproof membrane should moreover always be installed beneath the thermal insulation and over the concrete.

The above mentioned materials can also be used to insulate concrete structures supporting paved areas forming the roofs of underground car parks and like buildings. When used between a concrete structure and paving, they also diminish solar effects by reducing temperature fluctuations in the concrete and the consequential movements therein.

The simplest method of insulating a ground floor slab is to fix vertical sheets around its perimeter as indicated in the previously mentioned Fig. 3/1. Greater insulation can be obtained by laying horizontal strips of insulating board (1-m wide) around the perimeter to butt up to the vertical sheets – see Fig. 3/2. Maximum insulation is obtained by covering the whole of the slab site (Fig. 3/3), or if preferred the whole of the hardcore area, suitably blinded with sand to prevent damage to the damp proof membrane and insulation boards. Although cellular plastics boards are not unduly compressed by normal floorloads and usually have sufficient compressive strength to carry normal site foot-traffic, some precautions should be taken during building operations, e.g. heavy loads which have to be taken over them, (like barrows filled with concrete,) should be moved over planks laid on the surface of the boards.

The compressive strength of these cellular plastics, and hence the acceptable practical loading, depends on their bulk density. Expanded polystyrene at 16 kg/m^3 bulk density will carry a load of 1200 kg/m^2 indefinitely without compression. At 40 kg/m^3 density, this loading is about 3600 kg/m^2. Expanded polyurethane at the normally produced density of 32 kg/m^3, or expanded ebonite at 64 kg/m^3, will also carry about the same loads.

Material costs vary: expanded polystyrene is the cheapest, rigid vulcanised natural rubber (ebonite) the most expensive, at the bulk densities normally used in general building.

Floor loadings in cold-storage houses are generally much higher than those in other industrial or domestic premises. Any of the three expanded plastics just mentioned can be used for the floor insulation of cold stores, except that the expanded polystyrene should have a bulk density of 32 kg/m^3 in order to carry the high loadings involved. Cellular plastics with higher densities are also available for insulating column bases in this type of building. Their use to insulate the heat bridge formed by the column base is fully justified even though the insulation properties are slightly reduced by the higher densities.

Expanded plastics have advantages over conventional materials for floor insulation in that they are resistant to moisture, moulds and fungi, and can withstand floor loadings for indefinite periods without any compression and loss of insulation efficiency.

2. *Acoustic insulation*

The inclusion of a layer of resilient cellular plastics under a floor screed reduces the transmission of impact sound through a floor, but has little effect on sound transmission through the structural framework of a building. The mass law cannot be applied but noise transmission is reduced mainly because the sound energy is absorbed by the air in the cells of the cellular material. There are many variations in the different types of cellular plastics used for such purposes (as well as in the constructions available) so that reliable sound reduction factors for them cannot be quoted.

3. *Vibration*

Cellular plastics, in the form of sheet and strips can readily be used round the edges of small machine beds etc., to prevent or reduce the transmission of structural borne vibrations.

(vii) *Pipes and ducts*

The use of plastics pipes for services is described in Section Eight. Plastics pipes made from polyethylene or from unplasticised PVC can however also be cast in building foundations as ducting for all service media. They have the advantage of being light and easily handled, and moreover can be easily cut and jointed to form runs of any required configuration; they also have an indefinite life.

Plastics ducts that are to be cast into concrete must be firmly secured in position before the concrete is placed, otherwise floatation can result. Services that generate heat (e.g. electric cables) *may* produce temperatures which can affect or under extreme conditions even soften or melt the thermoplastic material normally used for forming the ducts. Though this may be unimportant during ordinary service conditions, any melting of the ducts could for example make subsequent cable withdrawal difficult.

(viii) *Modifying properties of concrete by inclusion of plastics*

Polypropylene fibres have been used to modify the properties of set concrete; twisted fibres of this material are used for example, instead of conventional reinforcement, in concrete piles to increase impact resistance.

(ix) *Bolt boxes and formers*

Expanded polystyrene is an excellent material for making formers for pockets, holes and similar cavities in concrete. It is cheap and easily worked with simple wood-working tools, and can be removed from cavities in concrete by cutting or by burning, an operation which can be difficult when wooden formers have to be removed from cavities that are under-reamed or grooved.

When casting long bolt holes, the expanded polystyrene core should be anchored to prevent it moving during the pouring and vibrating of the concrete base.

EXTERNAL WALLS, ROOFS, DOORS AND WINDOWS

(a) Introduction

The various characteristics of plastics must be considered before they are selected as facings or as structural units for use in walls, roofs, doors or windows. Guidance on these matters and on the plastics suitable for various locations is given in the following sub-sections as well as in Tables 4/1 and 4/2.

The introduction of plastics has widened the scope of the durable coloured and textured materials available to architects and designers. Their properties moreover are often superior to those of other materials, although it is only after the duties of a particular construction have been established, that a selection of its component materials can be made to give the best results.

Transparent, translucent and opaque plastics sheets complying with the appropriate British Standard have good weather resistant properties. They can be used either self supporting (usually as profiled sheets) or as coatings on other materials to improve appearance or to increase durability. The coatings may be applied during manufacture as a film or liquid, by roller, spray or brush methods.

Cellular plastics, owing to their good thermal insulating characteristics provide excellent insulation for external walls and roofs, though they are not generally suitable for exposure to the weather.

(b) External Walls

(i) *Profiled metal sheets with plastics coatings*

Plastics coatings are generally used to protect and to enhance the appearance of sheet steel galvanised in accordance with B.S. 2989 (Hot-Dip Galvanised Plain Steel Sheet and Coil). Such coatings provide various surface textures and also offer an attractive range of colours. Special colours can be supplied but whenever possible purchasers should use the standard colours recommended by the suppliers since the results of exposing untested colour shades are unpredictable.

Film coatings to sheet surfaces are usually of PVC, normally about 0.25-mm thick, being generally applied to metal strip by a continuous process in the factory. Polyvinyl fluoride film can be used, but is not made in the U.K., and is not widely available on a commercial scale.

Plastisol and organosal coatings are usually the most durable of the liquid applied types, and when dry as a film are about 0.25-mm and 0.75-mm thick respectively. Both types are roller applied and require stoving – these processes therefore being carried out in the factory.

Epoxy resins, in conjunction with alkyd, vinyl and acrylic materials are used to increase the adhesive qualities of the coatings; they are also used with phenolic resins as a laquer having high chemical resistance. These laquers can be used to coat the reverse sides of steel sheets galvanised to B.S. 2989 and finished on the exposed sides with other plastics coatings.

TABLE 4/1:   CHARACTERISTICS OF PLASTICS-COATED METAL SHEETS

(1)	(2)	(3)	(4)	(5)	(6)	(7)
Property	Profiled steel sheets galvanized to B.S. 2989 with PVC film	Profiled aluminium sheet with PVC film	Steel sheets galvanised to B.S. 2989 with plastisol or organosol coatings	Aluminium sheets with plastisol or organosol coatings	Steel sheets galvanised to B.S. 2989 with alkyd, acrylic or vinyl coating	Aluminium sheets with alkyd, acrylic or vinyl coating
Resistance to weather	*Very Good:* Correct fixings of sheets to rails together with side and end lap fixings must be used. PVC tapes to be used on rail faces or similar precautions taken to prevent metal contact and consequent electrolytic corrosion.				Fixings should be stainless steel or plastic covered to prevent corrosion.	
Durability	*Good:* High resistance to atmospheric pollution		*Good:* Better resistance to deterioration by atmospheric acids than other liquid applied coatings		*Fair:* Can be used for external surfaces. Excellent decorative finish for internal surfaces	
Strength	*Non Load Bearing:* Wind loading depends on degree of exposure. Permissible spans of sheets depends upon arrangement of sheets, profile section, gauge of metal and limits on deflection. Used as structural element for lightweight metal deck roofs to support insulation layer and bitumen felt weatherproof membrane					
Structural weight	*Light:*	Even if used with insulating lining				
Resistance to damage	Although steel sheets are more resistant than aluminium to indentation and tearing when subject to impact, it is usually necessary to provide plinth walls of brick or similar construction in locations where damage may occur. Coatings will scratch but galvanizing of steel and oxidation of aluminium helps prevent spread of corrosion. Coatings remain bonded to sheets bent by impact. Sheets will not shatter under impact					
Forming characteristics	Sheets usually formed after film applied. Preferable for cutting and forming to be carried out at works and not on site		Highly flexible coatings available especially plastisols enabling sharp bends to be made without film cracking. Sheets formed after coatings applied		Vinyls are more flexible than acrylics and alkyds and are most suitable for sheets formed after coating. Alkyds are very durable and suitable for coating preformed sheets	
Appearance	Pleasing effects obtained by use of colours and profiles. Embossed finishes available		Pleasing effects obtained by use of colours and profiles. Embossed finishes available on plastisol coated sheets		Pleasing effects obtained by use of colours and profiles	
Thermal insulation	*Poor:* Single sheet cladding has high thermal transmission characteristics and insulation lining must be provided.					
Sound insulation	*Poor:* Sound insulating properties improved by use of thermal insulating lining					
Fire characteristics (flame spread)	Flame spread ratings vary from Class 1 to Class 2 depending on material and supplier		Flame spread from Class 1 to Class 2 depending on material and supplier		Class 1 rating can be obtained for vinyl and acrylic coated sheets	
Erection considerations	Very rapid erection is possible with these forms of cladding. Consideration should be given to fixings such as self-tapping screws which require access from one side only especially when access to internal face is difficult					
Maintenance	Coating with air-drying films may be required – Period before coating will depend on environment. There may be difficulty in maintaining these ...		Coating with air-drying films may be required – Period before coating will depend on environment		It is anticipated that recoating with air-drying paints will be required, the period between installation and re-painting depending upon the environment	

TABLE 4/2: CHARACTERISTICS OF PLASTICS SHEETS

(1) Property	(2) Extruded PVC sheets to B.S. 4203	(3) Glass-reinforced plastics sheet to B.S. 4154	(4) Acrylic sheet
Resistance to weather	*Good:* Correct fixings of sheets to rails together with side and end lap fixings must be used		
Durability	*Fair:* Minimum life of ten years but longer life can be expected in most locations	*General Purpose – Good:* A reduction in light transmission can be expected. *S.E.:* Has poorer durability than G.P. Grade, can be as little as ten years	*Good:* Experience indicates a minimum of 40-year life.
Strength	*Non Load Bearing:* Wind loading depends on exposure. Span of sheeting depends on arrangement of sheets, profile section, gauge of sheet and permissible deflection		
Structural weight	*Extremely light*		
Resistance to damage	Less resistant to impact damage at low temperatures	Resistant to minor impact damage	Low resistance to impact damage at all normal temperatures
Forming characteristics	Can be obtained to suit most standard profiles of steel, aluminium and asbestos sheeting		
Appearance	Pleasing effects obtained using tinted sheets and arrangement of profiles		
Thermal insulation	Low 'U' values		
Sound insulation	*Poor:*		
Light transmission values for transparent grades	UPVC, 85% UPVC/wire laminate, 75%	Standard Grade, 87% S.E. Grade, 83%	92%
Fire characteristics Flame spread B.S. 476 Part 1	UPVC – Class 1 UPVC/wire laminate – Class 1	Standard Grade – Class 2 S.E. Grade – Class 1	Class 3
Fire rating B.S. 476 Part 3	UPVC – – UPVC/wire laminate – AA	Standard Grade – AD S.E. Grade – AA	
Erection considerations	Rapid erection possible, care must be taken to allow for relatively large temperature movements	Rapid erection possible	Rapid erection possible. Provision must be made for relatively large temperature movements
Maintenance	Wash with water and detergent	Wash with water and detergent	Cracks can be repaired with cement and surface polished. May be washed with soap and water – organic cleaners should not be used.
Remarks			Surface may be treated with anti-static solution to reduce static which attracts dust

Such coatings on the reverse side reduce the risk of corrosion in the interstices formed by laps in the sheets. Alkyd, vinyl, acrylic and phenolic coatings are roller applied, though vinyls and acrylics can be applied to preformed sheets by spray.

The control possible only with factory application produces more uniform and consistent coatings than can be obtained with on-site painting. In the factory, first class preparation of metal (sheet) surfaces can be carried out by special equipment (forming part of the continuous coating plant) at a fraction of the cost of the less effective site preparation. None of these application processes relies on stoving as such, but many depend on controlled heat to the coating material, the rollers and to the surfaces in order to produce sound coatings − it is not practical to ensure such control with site painting, and factory applied coatings are cheaper and better.

Sheets with certain factory-applied coatings may subsequently have to be formed. The radii to which they may be bent depends on the coatings; some of these are more flexible than others and permit bending to smaller radii without cracking or delamination. Plastisol coatings are very flexible but acrylics and alkyds are not.

As well as being used for exterior surfaces, finishes of this type may also be applied to metal facings on the surface of insulation panels or of single-skin sheeting and other similar interior surfaces; though coatings of the alkyd, vinyl, and acrylic types are generally employed for such applications.

Factory-applied surface coatings are more prone to damage whilst sheets or panels are being handled during transport or erection, but as they are better and cheaper than site applied finishes, the resultant savings in cost and maintenance generally warrant the extra care needed during handling, especially during erection. Factory-applied finishes also have an advantage in that when "inside" surfaces are treated, the coating covers areas in contact with any supporting rails etc.

It can be difficult however to obtain small quantities of factory-finished sheeting and accessories if stocks are low, it being more economic for manufacturers to produce comparatively large batches once their equipment has been set up for a particular run. Difficulties may also be met if special colours are required in small quantities.

(ii) *Composites of coated metal sheets and insulation*

Plastics coated steel or aluminium sheets can be used independently or with some form of insulation for the external cladding of buildings, of which a recent development is the use of cellular polyurethane or polystyrene core between two metal sheets. Core thickness can be made to suit the degree of insulation required. A good bond between core and sheet can be obtained when polyurethane is foamed in situ, or by using a core of preformed polystyrene with an adhesive. These composities function as complete structural units and have superior structural properties to those of separate external cladding sheets with internal lining. More attention however must be given to the design of weatherproof joints, since the greater thickness of the composites does not enable the conventional longitudinal and transverse lap joints (common for thin gauge sheets) to be used.

A proprietary cladding of this composite type, embodying a joint with a concealed aluminium extruded spline, is depicted in Fig. 4/1. In this, the aluminium facing material is flanged to fit into the spline and is sealed with a neoprene extrusion; a typical corner detail is shown in Fig. 4/2. This type of

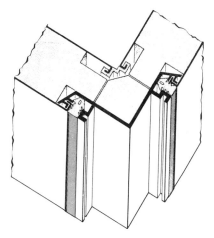

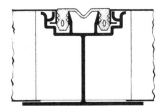

Fig. 4/1 Weatherproof composite joint — with concealed aluminium spline sealed by a neoprene extrusion.

Fig. 4/2 Corner detail of composite joint shown in Fig. 4/1.

cladding may be fixed to its sheeting rails by means of a "T" shaped spline secured to the rails before the panels are placed in position (Fig. 4/3), or as described in the paragraph below. Lap joints may be used especially where cladding of this type has a profiled sheet on the exterior face, and a flat sheet on the inner. Jointing technique usually involves the setting back of

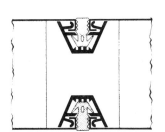

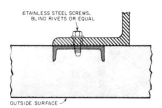

Fig. 4/3 Use of T-shaped spline for securing cladding to sheeting rails (see also Figs 4/1 and 4/2).

Fig. 4/4 Concealed fixing using a channel in plastics cored panel to provide extra strength.

the insulation to enable the external sheet to form the lap. Cutting the sheet on site is therefore not practicable, and all sheets should be purpose made. Where building design permits, long sheets should be used in order to avoid or minimise cross jointing.

Composite cladding may be fixed to sheeting rails by through bolts or by concealed fixings using blind rivets; self-tapping screws from the inside of a building may also be used. Fig. 4/4 indicates a typical concealed fixing using a channel (or wooden block) in the panel to provide extra strength.

Other composites consist of profiled galvanised steel or aluminium sheets with plastics coatings (conforming to those described in (i) above)*, bonded to polyurethane foam 12.5, 19.0, or 25.4-mm thick, usually with a paper finish on the inside surface. The paper lining may be kraft paper similar to that used for plasterboard and suitable for site painting, or plastics coated paper with a 'self-finish'.

(iii) *Glass reinforced plastics sheets (GRP Sheets)*

Sheets made from thermosetting polyester resins reinforced with glass fibre mat or chopped glass fibre are produced to suit most standard profiles of asbestos cement, steel and aluminium sheeting. They are made to comply

Fig. 4/5 Long length of glass-reinforced plastics profiled sheeting being installed as transparent roofing material.

with B.S. 4154 Corrugated Plastics Translucent Sheets Made from Thermo-setting Polyester Resins (Glass-Fibre Reinforced), normally by a continuous process. Notwithstanding transport and handling difficulties which limit the lengths that may be conveniently used, lengths longer than 12-m are not uncommon. Fig. 4/5 shows a 22-m length of GRP profiled sheeting being used on the roof of a new Physical Training building. Flat GRP sheets can also be supplied.

* Aluminium and sheets with a mill finish are also available.

Transparent, translucent or opaque sheets can also be obtained, tinting pigments being used in the translucent or opaque types to provide colours that may be required.

B.S. 4154 also gives useful information on the applications methods of fixing, durability, as well as on the optical properties and other details of this sheeting material.

The plastics used in the manufacture of these sheets resist many chemicals such as dilute acids and alkalis and those in industrial atmospheres; they are however liable to attack by some organic solvents and the manufacturers advice on this should be sought. Sheets on typical buildings under normal conditions have given satisfactory service for more than ten years, though there is a tendency for the external surfaces "to weather". This weathering exposes the fibres and reduces light transmission, especially when dirt collects on the roughened surface. The ultra-violet component in sunlight is the main cause of this degradation, the rate of which is a function of the materials' exposure to sunlight. Pigments which absorb ultra-violet light reduce the rate of deterioration.

Sheets can be obtained with a film of polyvinyl fluoride on the exposed face, and it is claimed that such sheets have better weather resistant properties.

GRP sheets can also be supplied manufactured from resins containing additives which give improved fire-retardent properties. Class 1 flame-spread characteristics, complying with Part 1 (Fire Tests on Building Materials and Structures) of B.S. 476, can be achieved with those usually classified as S.E. grade (i.e. self-extinguishing). Standard grades are recommended where fire-retardent properties are not required since the additives in the S.E. grades may reduce durability. The standard grades usually have a Class 2 flame-spread characteristic.

The requirements of individual insurance companies have sometimes limited the maximum area over which this type of sheet may be used; such requirements should, therefore, be checked at the design stage.

Single-length sheets for glazing are sometimes preferred since they avoid the use of cross joints which collect dirt and so form a dark streak across a glazed panel. Similar streaks also appear in longitudinal joints, but are less noticeable since such joints are narrower and parallel to the corrugations.

Low thermal transmission cannot be obtained by adding thermal insulating materials when sheets are used for daylight lighting. To reduce heat loss and to minimise or prevent condensation in such cases, several proprietary methods have been developed and are available — all use double sheeting enclosing an insulating air space.

If light transmission is unimportant, however, wall-type units comprising cellular plastics cores faced externally with GRP sheets may be employed. These units combine the thermal insulating properties of the cores with the impermeable and aesthetic properties of the sheets; colouring and relief obtainable with the glass-reinforced plastics facing can provide a pleasing appearance.

(iv) *Extruded unplasticised PVC sheets (UPVC Sheets)*

Sheets of this type, complying with B.S. 4203 (Extruded Rigid PVC Corrugated Sheeting) can be obtained with profiles to suit most asbestos-cement, steel and aluminium sheets. UPVC is a thermoplastic, the sheets being produced by extrusion processes which allows them to be used in long lengths. The material has a high coefficient of expansion and precautions must be taken, especially with long sheets, to permit expansion and contraction to take place freely. Otherwise the sheets or their fixings fail. Flat rigid PVC sheets can also be supplied.

Transparent sheets may also be obtained, and if required, tinting pigments can be introduced during manufacture. Useful information relating to the

Fig. 4/6 Unplasticised PVC corrugated sheeting as roof and walls of a swimming pool.

applications of this sheeting material, its durability, fixing methods, as well as its optical properties and temperature restrictions is given in B.S. 4203.

Under normal conditions, opaque sheets and transparent sheets can be expected to have a minimum life of about 15 and 10 years respectively, though transparent sheets tend to become opaque as they age.

UPVC tends to soften when heated. It is self-extinguishing, however, with a Class 1 flame spread classification and will collapse before it ignites. This characteristic is useful when the material is employed in a fire ventilator.

As with GRP sheets, single-lengths are preferable for glazing panels in order to avoid dirt streaks at horizontal laps. Fig. 4/6 illustrates the use of UPVC corrugated sheeting as roof and walls of a swimming pool.

UPVC wire laminates each consisting of a layer of reinforcing wire mesh between two layers of plastic sheets are also available. Because of the wire mesh, there is a greater resistance to collapse in a fire than with the unreinforced UPVC sheets, though the mesh usually reduces light transmission. For commonly available transparent PVC sheets, the light transmission is about 85%, but this is reduced to 75% when wire reinforcement is used.

Extruded unplasticised PVC, in the form of traditional weather boarding is made in a range of colours and requires no maintenance. Potential users should, however, check and be satisfied in regard to colour fastness, weather resistance and the fixing arrangements necessary to allow for thermal movement.

(v) *Acrylic sheets*

Acrylic sheets have better light transmission properties than any other plastics. Twenty years experience has also proved that they have excellent weathering properties. The material itself, however, has a higher flame spread classification than other similar plastics and is more expensive. It is at present used mainly for transparent light domes, decorative panels and the like.

(vi) *Infill panels to curtain walls*

Most manufacturers of curtain wall construction now use plastics fo: infill panels. Resin-bonded plywood, faced with decorative plastics films of various types, are used for panels having separate thermal insulation linings. Alternatively, if higher thermal insulation is required, cellular plastics can be used as the base for the panels.

Steel and aluminium sheets, with the films and plastics coatings referred to in Section Four (b) (i), are available in flat or pressed form for infill panels.

Asbestos board and asbestos insulation board can be used with finishes of melamine, formaldehyde, reinforced polyester, filled epoxy and similar plastics. If some form of architectural relief is required, single-skin panels manufactured from reinforced polyester can be obtained.

Several proprietary boards are available for use as infill panels. They usually comprise a cellular plastics core, (generally polystyrene or polyurethane), those for external wall panels are faced externally with weather-resistant facing such as aluminium or protected steel. A vapour barrier is necessary on the internal face of panels used externally.

Because of the many types of fixings and methods of bedding panels, manufacturers of curtain wall cladding should be consulted when selecting a particular infill panel.

(vii) *Wall cladding units to framed buildings*

Wall units are now being developed with external facings of glass-reinforced plastics, the panels being made in single units for cladding external faces of buildings. The panels are produced with the colouring and architectural finish to suit the external face; windows are fitted as required, and insulation provided by lightweight concrete or other materials. The units can have a dry finish suitable for decorating or be provided with a self-finish on the internal face.

The economies of this type of wall cladding become apparent when large numbers of panels of a similar type can be manufactured, for the initial costs are usually fairly high. It generally follows, as with many articles manufactured from plastics materials, that unit costs fall as the quantity required increases. Fig. 4/7 shows a typical building with GRP panels moulded with bold projections and lipped edges; the panels being about 2-m wide x 6-m high x 2-mm thick. They are butt jointed, the lipped edges being bolted together and to the structural members. A compressible plastic filler in the butt joints prevents the passage of water and allows for movement in the panels. (It is claimed that this construction conforms with Section E of The Building Regulations.) Such panels

Fig. 4/7 Building with glass-reinforced plastics panels (moulded) as facing.

can be designed to suit individual requirements, and their use can provide an economic facing system if some 100 or more panels are used.

Some advantages of this type of wall cladding are: —

1. A clean appearance.
2. Surfaces can be readily cleaned.
3. Lightness and quick assembly.
4. Good resistance to atmospheric attack.

The panels tend to become dirty during building operations, but as just indicated, can be easily cleaned on completion.

(viii) *Cellular plastics*

Cellular plastics materials are good thermal insulators, and are generally unaffected by fungi, vermin, insects and moisture. The cellular form is usually produced by: —

1. Mechanical frothing of the resin using air.
2. Release of a gas or vapour from a low boiling point liquid absorbed in the resin.
3. Incorporating an agent which releases a gas into the resin or polymer when the temperature is increased or as result of chemical action.

Various aspects of thermal insulation are covered in Section Three (c) (vi). Basically, however, cellular plastics are used as insulating materials in the form of boards and other moulded or extruded sections, bonded to other elements if required. They are also supplied as liquids for spraying on to surfaces or for foaming in cavities in the construction; they are prepared near the final position and sprayed onto prepared surfaces or injected into a cavity or into shapes serving as permanent moulds in which foaming takes place.

Polyurethane, phenol formaldehyde or urea formaldehyde are the most common plastics for cavity filling on site. They are generally supplied in two-pack form, and , after mixing, can be injected through holes formed or drilled in the facing of walls. Cavities in new constructions, can be filled through openings left by the builder (in the top of the cavities). After the material has cured, it provides a structure with an extremely high resistance to moisture movement and with good thermal insulation. The introduction of the foam into cavities requires special equipment however, as well as experienced operators. Urea formaldehyde can be injected as a continuous process, but polyurethane requires to be divided into sections of about 1-metre square.

Tests indicate that the thermal transmission ("U" value in W/m^2 °C, — see Appendix C) of a cavity wall with 114-mm brick inner and outer skins, plastered internally and having a 50-mm cavity can be reduced from 1.7 with no cavity insulation to 0.6 with a cavity insulation of cellular plastics having a density of 8 kg/m^3.

Sprayed polyurethane foam can be applied to virtually any surface in order to increase the insulation properties of a wall or roof. It is equally suitable for new or existing work but as already indicated specialised application techniques are required and such work is best carried out by those specialising in these processes. Fig. 4/8 shows polyurethane foam being applied to the steel cladding of a building.

Care must be taken to prevent overspray since this can be a nuisance unless precautions are taken to mask or protect appropriate areas.

Care must also be exercised in the use of polyurethane foams on account of toxicity and flammability hazards. Only diphenylmethane diisocyanate, and not the more volatile toluene diisocyanate should be used when spraying foam (The local representative of the raw material supplier can be consulted about this). Operators if working in enclosed spaces should wear fresh-air hoods that completely cover the head. The set foam is flammable unless suitable additivies are incorporated, or unless the sprayed surface is covered by an unbroken fire-retardant coating. There is also a risk of spontaneous combustion if the mixing ratio is wrong, or if a thick layer is built up too quickly for the heat of chemical reaction to be safely dissipated. There are, however, some polyurethane foam spraying systems which do not present a spontaneous combustion hazard when the mixing ratio differs from the prescribed figure.

Boards made from cellular plastics are usually manufactured from:—

Expanded polystyrene	Polyvinyl chloride
Extruded expanded polystyrene	Phenolformaldehyde
Polyurethane	Ebonite

Fig. 4/8 Polyurethane foam being sprayed on to steel cladding.

Boards are made by an expansion process, being cut to the required thickness after foaming, or by extrusion which produces finished boards of the required thickness. Polyurethane boards are normally produced with a kraft or plastics-coated paper on the face, though other surfacing materials (e.g. plasterboard) are available. Polystyrene and polyurethane boards, because of their low price, are the most widely used in the building industry.

Generally, the physical properties of foamed or cellular plastics are related to density, the higher densities usually being associated with greater strength and lower thermal insulation. Most manufacturers publish information on the thermal transmission values (k-values), and these are generally within the range 0.017 to 0.036 W/m deg C.

(ix) *Accessories*

Screws, hook bolts, bolts and nuts, self-tapping screws, cartridge-fired pins, drive screws and similar fixings are available for securing plastics coated profiled zinc-coated steel or aluminium sheets to a building frame.

Similar fixings are also used for glass-reinforced plastics and PVC profiled sheets, (excepting cartridge fired pins which tend to shatter these sheets, at the fixing points). The type of fixing depends largely on the frame materials.

Fig. 4/9 Plastics capped fittings.

Washers and caps manufactured from plastics help to make a weathertight seal at the fixing, and make this as durable as the sheeting. They also improve its appearance, and to some extent reduce the cold-bridge effect of the fixing. They are available in many forms and may consist of plastics mouldings which clip or screw on to the external part of the completed fixing (as in the case of a nut and projecting part of a hook bolt or as a moulded head of a self-tapping screw). They are available in colours to suit the plastics coating of the sheet, typical fittings of this type being depicted in Fig. 4/9.

In order to reduce the possibility of corrosion in crevices between the surfaces of the sheets and the structure, an insulating layer should be provided especially where electrolytic corrosion may result from the contact of plain aluminium and steel. Paint or other insulating film may be applied to the sheet or steel surfaces for this purpose, but adhesive PVC tapes applied to the steelwork surfaces provide a more durable and effective insulation layer.

Cellular plastics sections are available in a variety of forms to close the gaps between profiled sheets and wall or frame surfaces. They are usually about 50-mm wide and secured by adhesive to the wall or frame and sheet.

(c) Sloping Roofs Incorporating Lap-Jointed Sheets

Factors arising from the construction of the roof are dealt with under two headings as follows:

(i) *Sloping roof constructions*

The types of roof referred to, are normally constructed from profiled sheets and rely on a slope to shed water, continuous waterproof membranes not being provided. Laps at end and side joints of the sheets are arranged to exclude water. Gaskets, additional fixings and seam bolting are sometimes used to help prevent driving rain from entering the building, (especially if a flat pitch is used). The degree of water-tightness, however, depends largely on the slope as well as on the size of the lap at the end and side of the sheets, and upon the shape of the corrugations forming the side laps.

Most of the profiled sheets, and insulation materials referred to in Section Four (b) are also suitable for sloping roofs. Similar fixings and other accessories can also be used.

(ii) *Roof slope (pitch) and sealing*

Sheeting laid in the manner just described can be used with slopes varying from as little as 5° to the horizontal up to vertical wall cladding applications. The flatter the pitch, however, the more attention must be given to joint sealing, to prevent ingress of driving rain and snow.

Long sheets spanning ridge to eaves obviate the risk of leakage at cross joints; if not excessively long, they are cheaper and improve the appearance of the roof. An increase in the number of corrugations in the side laps on longitudinal joints of roof sheeting also increases the weather resistance of the roof. Alternatively, gaskets may be used to seal both cross and longitudinal joints, preformed plastic strips or compound being used as the gasket material. When gaskets are used, there must be a sufficient number of fixings in the cross joints, as well as seam bolts or rivets in the longitudinal joints, to maintain the sheets in contact with the gasket.

(d) Flat or Sloping Roofs Incorporating Continuous Waterproof Layers

Relevant factors under this heading are dealt with under six items as below:—

(i) *Components*

The components of roofs of this type usually include:—

1. Structural deck.
2. Vapour barrier.
3. Insulation board.
4. Weatherproofing membrane.

In addition there are accessories, including various types of mechanical fixings, adhesives, roof trims and other similar items in which plastics are usefully incorporated in the construction.

Although the description of a particular component may indicate its primary function, other properties are also required, e.g. an insulation layer should have some structural strength in order that it can support a weatherproofing membrane. A vapour barrier for example can strengthen an insulation layer by acting as a reinforcement. All aspects must, therefore, be considered if the best results are to be obtained from plastics materials in such applications.

(ii) *Structural decks*

The creep characteristics and structural properties of plastics materials render them unsuitable for use as roof decks. The more common types of roof deck are made from reinforced concrete, (in situ or as precast slabs), timber joists and boards, wood wool and similar slabs, asbestos panels, profiled steel and aluminium sheets or any number of similar constructions.

Steel and aluminium profiled sheets protected with plastics as described in Section Four (b) (i) are used extensively for roof decks. Structural decks made from profiled aluminium are often left uncoated, especially in industrial buildings or in buildings where a suspended ceiling is provided. Some form of coating is generally used on the underside of steel decks, however, to help the galvanising resist corrosion. The plastisol and PVC film coatings referred to in Section Four (b) (i) are generally too expensive for this purpose but organosal, alkyd or one of the acrylic or vinyl finishes can be used. These finishes can also be applied to aluminium when this is selected for the decking.

Plastics caps to the mechanical fixings securing metal decks to the supporting frame are not so important as with wall cladding, since trough fixings are protected by the weather-proofing membrane.

PVC tapes are also used to prevent corrosion between decking and the purlins as in the case of wall cladding.

(iii) *Vapour barriers*

Reinforced bitumen felts are normally used as a vapour barrier for the insulation board in metal deck roofs. This is because they are compatible with the hot bitumen adhesive used to bond the vapour barrier to the deck, and the insulation board to the vapour barrier.

Plastics film (i.e. polyethylene and plasticised PVC sheets) is used as a vapour barrier to insulation boards in roofs of concrete or other rigid constructions.

(iv) *Insulation boards*

Cellular plastics boards made from expanded polystyrene, rigid polyurethane or polyvinyl chloride may be used as insulation boards on all types of roofs: The characteristics of these boards are described in Section Four (b) (viii). Rigid polyurethane boards are usually supplied with a plain or bituminized kraft paper facing, or can be obtained with a layer of bitumen felt bonded to one side.

Insulation board may be supported by a flat surface as with concrete and similar roof construction, or by a series of closely spaced ribs formed by profiled metal decks. This, together with the deflection characteristics of the roof must be taken into account when selecting the type of board. The structural properties of a vapour barrier are more important in a metal deck roof.

Figure 4/10 shows a cellular plastics insulation board used with a typical profiled metal structural roof deck. A similar type of board may be used on a concrete roof to provide insulation; polystyrene, cut from large blocks, can be supplied in wedge form to provide the necessary falls to a flat concrete slab,

Fig. 4/10 Cellular plastics insulation board as used on profiled metal roof deck.

thus obviating wet screeds or other measures necessary if a parallel thickness board is used. Extruded boards or parallel cut boards of uniform thickness are available for use with metal deck of similar structural units which can be laid to falls by fillets or other fairly simple measures.

Flexible cellular plastics usually have an "open cell" structure and rigid cellular plastics boards a "closed cell" structure. The latter offers greater resistance to permeability by water vapour diffusion. (See Table 4/3) Cellular

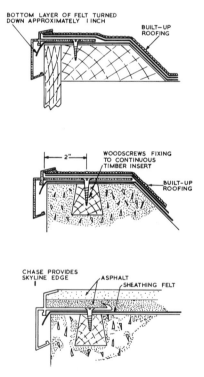

Fig. 4/11 Glass-reinforced plastics verge trims (with various finishes) on concrete or timber roof decks.

plastics boards for roof and wall applications are generally of the rigid foam type.

TABLE 4/3: PROPERTIES OF SOME CELLULAR PLASTICS

Cellular material	Density Kg/m³	Permeability to water vapour diffusion. g/m² 24 h at 38°C, 90% R.H. 50-mm thick
Expanded polystyrene	16.0	70
Foamed urea-formaldehyde (site foamed)	3.2 to 12.8	Less than 30
Foamed polyurethane (flexible)	32.0	Very high
Foamed polyurethane (rigid)	32.0	Less than 2.5

Most cellular plastics are permeable to some degree, and the provision of a vapour barrier is recommended when they are used as insulation in environments exposing them continually to high relative humidities. Under drier conditions, the vapour barrier may be omitted (as a moisture barrier) provided that the increased strength it gives to the insulation boards on metal deck roofs is deemed unnecessary.

If the weight of that part of the roof construction above the insulation board is insufficient to resist suction pressures, some method of bonding the insulation board to the structural deck or vapour barrier is necessary. Screws or other fixings may be used or the board secured by adhesive. Although various types of adhesives are available, hot bitumen bonding compound is most commonly used. Thermosetting plastics boards, such as polyurethane, especially when faced with kraft paper, are relatively unaffected by the temperature of hot bitumen. Thermoplastic cellular boards, however, melt at a lower temperature than that of hot bitumen, so that bitumen compounds cannot be directly applied to them. Indirect methods of applying the hot bitumen to the other surfaces and bedding the board into the bitumen as it cools must be used.

Other types of adhesive are available for securing insulation board, but these are usually more affected by adverse weather and poor application conditions — and, experience so far, indicates that the resulting adhesion is inferior to that obtained with hot bitumen.

The kraft paper facing to polyurethane boards helps to make them fairly rigid. If the paper is stripped from one face, the boards become more pliable and can be used successfully as insulation to the curved surfaces of shell roofs and similar constructions. 12-mm thick boards can be bent to a radius of less than 300-mm without cracking.

(v) *Weatherproofing membranes*

The plastics and rubber materials listed below are available for weather-proofing membranes:—

> Neoprene rubber sheeting
> Butyl rubber sheeting
> Polyisobutylene sheeting
> Vinyl sheeting
> Vinyl asbestos sheeting
> Vinyl sheeting on bitumen felt

Weatherproofing systems of this type usually consist of a single sheet, generally about 1.3-mm thick, sometimes reinforced with hessian, glass fibre or similar material, the sheets being laid with lap or taped joints in a suitable adhesive. The sheeting can be laid on to insulation board, timber, wood-slabs and similar surfaces or direct on to concrete roofs if the surfaces are trowelled to a smooth finish. It is advisable to use a screed if concrete has a rough finish. Some systems require an adhesive for bonding the sheet to the base, different from that used for sealing the joints. Greater skill by the operative is needed with such systems to ensure that adhesive does not spread beyond the limits of the joint. Systems that use a common adhesive for bonding the sheet to the base and for sealing the joints are preferable.

The main advantages claimed for these weatherproofing membranes over bitumen felt is their greater resistance to penetration, damage and cracking (owing to their elastic properties). Good acid and alkali resistance is also claimed. With roofs finished with some of these materials, an AA rating in accordance with "Part Three — External Fire Exposure Roof Tests" of B.S. 476 may be obtained if the correct roof construction is used.

Existing bitumen felt and asphalt roof can be repaired with these membrane materials provided that deterioration is not advanced and a reasonable surface can be obtained for laying the sheeting.

With the neoprene rubber-based materials, it is advisable to provide a final seal coat by applying a brush coat of rubber based material over the surface of the sheeting after laying. Colour can be incorporated in this rubber based material if required. The seal coat helps to prevent degradation due to solar radiation and should be renewed at intervals of about fifteen/twenty years.

Certain adhesives are incompatible with different sheeting and base materials, and the manufacturers should be consulted when using these weatherproofing membranes.

(vi) *Gutters*

Rainwater can be removed from flat roofs by means of outlets set in the roof, water falling on the roof being led by falls to the outlets. Alternatively, a roof may be laid to fall to gutters where the storm water is collected and fed to the gutter outlets. Plate and sheet gutters in galvanised steel or aluminium can be used with this type of roof. It is more usual, however, to construct the gutters (when required) in a similar way to the roof, i.e. the insulation and weatherproof membrane is continued down the sides and across the soffit of the gutter to ensure a completely watertight construction to safeguard against overflow in the event of any stoppage of the gutter outlet.

(e) Accessories for Sloping and Flat Roofs

In addition to the tapes, fixings and adhesives, plastics have many other uses, some typical applications being as below:—

(i) *Extruded unplasticised PVC and GRP verge trims*

Typical details of GRP verge trims used with various combinations of bitumen felt or asphalt finishes together with concrete or timber roof decks are shown in Fig. 4/11.

(ii) *Fascia gutters*

Proprietory types of fascia gutters for use with flat or sloping roofs are referred to in Section Eight: Services. Glass-reinforced plastics gutters are now being considered for the larger box type of gutter normally used on industrial buildings.

(iii) *Glass-reinforced plastics flashings*

A typical apron flashing moulded in glass-reinforced plastics, and the method of incorporation in a typical wall construction is depicted in Figs. 4/12 and 4/13. This type of flashing can be supplied with purpose-made

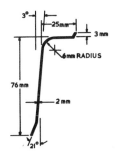
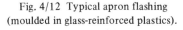
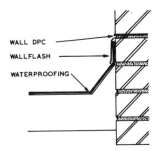

Fig. 4/12 Typical apron flashing (moulded in glass-reinforced plastics).

Fig. 4/13 Incorporation of apron flashing (Fig. 4/12) in a wall.

internal and external angles. A special type of lap joint is generally used to prevent it becoming detached.

(iv) *Pipe flashings*

These can be manufactured from glass-reinforced plastics where the flashing comes into contact with hot asphalt as with the flat roof shown in Fig. 4/14. With a pitched roof, as in Fig. 4/15, it is more common to use a more flexible material for the collar, e.g. neoprene. In all cases the vent skirt is usually made from unplasticised PVC.

(v) *Roof outlets*

Outlets connecting the rainwater pipes to the roof can be obtained manufactured from unplasticised PVC or glass-reinforced plastics. A typical roof

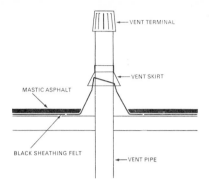

Fig. 4/14 Pipe flashing in a flat roof.   Fig. 4/15 Pipe flashing in a sloping roof.

outlet is shown in Fig. 4/16. This type of fitting gives the best results when
the outlet flange and spigot pipe are made from glass-reinforced plastics, to
prevent distortion resulting from the contact with hot asphalt or bitumen.
The ground guard and extension pipe, which need not be highly resistant to
heat, can be made from unplasticised PVC (UPVC). This type of fitting is equall
suitable for a flat roof or box gutter if required.

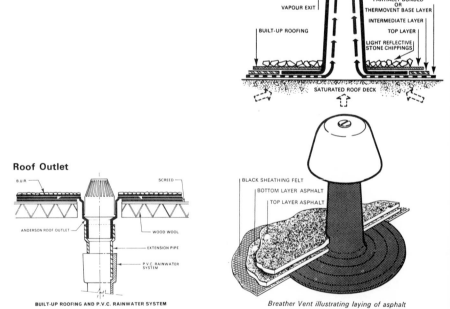

Fig. 4/16 Roof rainwater outlet.   Fig. 4/17 Typical plastics breather vent.

(vi) *Screed ventilators*

These fittings are used for drying out wet screeds in roofs. A typical fitting is illustrated in Fig. 4/17, having a base and flange made from glass-reinforced plastics to prevent distortion by hot asphalt, and a cap made from unplasticised PVC.

(f) External and Internal Doors

Factors under this heading are dealt with under the following seven items: —

(i) *Characteristics of doors*

When selecting components, plastics or otherwise, for parts of a door and frame, full consideration must be given to the function of the door. If used to give access through external walls, a door must be able to resist wind pressure or suction, and mechanical damage. It must also have the thermal insulation properties required for the particular position. If the door is not fully protected by a porch or similar structure, it should be weather resistant.

In many instances the larger part of the door has to be translucent or transparent, so as to avoid collisions or allow for natural illumination to the inside. The door also needs to have an appearance in keeping with its surroundings and in many cases fire resistance and acoustic properties are extremely important.

The characteristics needed for doors in internal walls are generally similar to those for doors in external walls, except that resistance to weather and to heat transmission are not usually required.

Door characteristics are not however determined solely by the above-mentioned factors; apart from the material(s) selected, the thermal and acoustic insulation between two faces of a door is influenced to a great extent by the degree of ccntact between the door and its frame. The sealing of the seam between the edges of the door and floor or door frame must also satisfy requirements of safety, strength and durability.

The closing of an opening in a wall can be effected in different ways, depending upon economics, size of opening required and the traffic passing through; hinged doors, revolving doors, sliding doors, etc., are all available.

(ii) *Flush doors*

Flush doors can be built up from a core of expanded polystyrene, polyurethane foam, wood or paper with a facing on both sides; the core provides insulation and rigidity. The facings, which may be of PVC, melamine-formaldehyde, wood, etc., should have a good appearance (flat, profiled, glossy, mat, coloured), be easy to clean and require minimum maintenance.

(iii) *Panelled doors*

Panelled doors usually comprise a frame, inside of which are the panels filled with a thin board construction. Frames are generally of timber. In the past panels have been of solid timber, plywood, hardboard and similar

materials; excellent results however can be obtained with melamine formaldehyde, unplasticised PVC or with other vinyl and similar faced materials which
can be set direct into grooves or rebates formed in the wooden frame, or
alternatively, fixed by means of unplasticised PVC extruded sections. A
section through a typical door using vinyl finished panels held in position by
wooden beads is shown in Fig. 4/18 which also depicts a similar section through

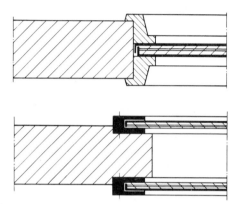

Fig. 4/18 Plastics-panelled door sections

> Top: Vinyl finished panels secured by wooden beads.
>
> Bottom: With unplasticised PVC extrusions and a double panel of vinyl finished
>   plywood.

a door with unplasticised PVC extrusions and a double panel of vinyl finished
plywood; in this the space between the panels can be filled with cellular plastics
to improve thermal and sound insulation properties.

(iv) *Glazed doors*

If a transparent or translucent door is required, unplasticised PVC or
acrylic flat sheet can be used to form a panel(s) in a timber-framed door.
These materials (especially unplasticised PVC) have certain advantages over
glass, in that they offer greater resistance to impact, and, even if failure
occurs, the resulting fragmentation is less dangerous than with glass. The
expansion characteristics of unplasticised PVC and acrylic usually necessitate
wider rebates than for glass, though these also help to prevent panels being
blown out as a result of flexing under high wind pressures.

(v) *Flexible doors*

Flexible doors, hung at the sides to open one way or to swing in both
directions to suit the flow of traffic, have proved useful for openings in walls
through which there is a constant traffic of small trucks. Such doors are
depicted in Fig. 4/19. They can be made entirely from plasticised PVC or
from rubber with panels of plasticised PVC for observation purposes — see lower
sketch. Flexible doors are also made with their lower halves of rubber, and with
their upper halves transparent. This type often has a rigid metal frame (consisting
only of a top rail and hanging stile), attached to the door frame by spring hinges.

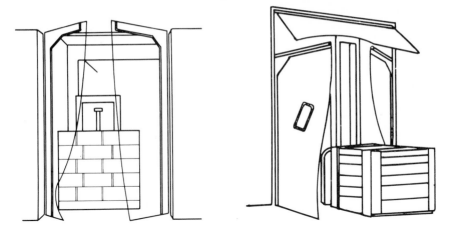

Fig. 4/19 Flexible plastic doors.

     Left: Flexible PVC door.

     Right: Flexible rubber door with PVC observation panel.

Flexible doors cannot be locked, so their use is restricted when security is essential.

Fig. 4/20 Flexible plastics door (for a conveyor shutter flap).

Figure 4/20 illustrates a small flexible door suitable for use in the opening where a conveyor passes through a wall.

(vi) *Sliding and lifting doors*

Sliding, folding and lifting doors can be made entirely of glass-reinforced plastic or from PVC. These materials can also be used as covering to a door framed from aluminium or similarly constructed. The doors can be provided with a flat finish or profiled effect to improve appearance and rigidity A typical glass-fibre reinforced plastic door in this category is shown in Fig. 4/21.

Fig. 4/21 Glass-fibre reinforced plastics door of the "up and over" type.

(vii) *Door accessories*

There are several accessories for doors using plastics materials, e.g.
Fig. 4/22 illustrates a typical extruded PVC section for use as lipping pieces
to the edge of flush doors. Nylon is now extensively used for washers in metal

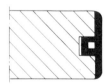

Fig. 4/22 Extruded PVC section as lipping for edges of plastics doors.

hinges, to reduce friction and lubrication, or for complete hinges. The Local
Authority should, however, be consulted before plastics hinges are used,
since these should not be employed in fire resistant or fire check doors.
Plastics components are also often used in several proprietary types of
sliding door gear.

Cellular plastics of the flexible foam, open-cell type are supplied in rolls,
the strip being pre-coated with adhesive and with a separating layer for use as
draught and weather excluders. It is an inexpensive self-adhesive and can be
quickly replaced after redecoration if required. Fig. 4/23 shows this type of

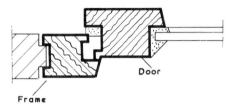

Fig. 4/23 Cellular self-adhesive weather excluding strips on door and frame of plastics with wood core.

sealer used in conjunction with a door and frame of plastics with a wood core.

(g) Windows

Factors relating to the application of plastics to windows are covered by the following seven items:—

(i) *Characteristics of windows*

Windows in external walls are usually provided for natural lighting and appearance though advantage is often taken to provide opening lights for controlled natural ventilation. In this Section reference is made only to the framed type of window; profiled transparent and translucent sheets are referred to in Section Twelve.

Windows are exposed to extreme differences between internal and external temperatures, to wind pressures, driving rain and condensation, as well as to the risk of mechanical damage during construction and whilst in service. They are usually made with some combination of fixed lights, vertical or horizontal pivoted sashes, and top, bottom or side hung sashes.

Plastics are generally used in windows either as:—

1. A substitute for glass as the glazing medium
2. Extruded plastics frames
3. Coverings to frames and sashes with wood or metal cores
4. Gaskets.

The main advantages of plastics over more traditional materials for window frames are: durability, resistance to mechanical damage and lower maintenance costs. Frames can be obtained in a range of colours and, as for other coloured plastics items, purchasers are advised to use the manufacturer's recommended colours and not insist on special colours.

Thermal expansion may be a problem, especially with dark colours, but can be reduced by using light coloured plastics materials. The problem is not so acute with plastics-covered metal or wood sections. Like other materials, plastics become dirty in industrial atmospheres and cleaning is necessary from time to time; this can be done when external window cleaning is carried out.

At present the costs of all-plastics windows is comparable with those of purpose-made anodised aluminium sections. Plastics-coated metal windows are more expensive.

Some windows illustrated in this section are manufactured in Europe and are not widely available in the United Kingdom.

(ii) *Plastics glazing*

Unplasticised PVC is available in sheets about 3-mm thick for glazing to windows, doors and similar locations. The material has high impact strength

Fig. 4/24 Exterior view of clear rigid PVC glazing.

and is particularly suitable when damage, accidental or wilful may be expected. A typical building with such glazing is illustrated in Fig. 4/24.

The usual method of fixing makes no allowance for expansion, and although this causes some bowing in hot weather, it eases the problem of sealing at the edges. It is essential for the sheets to be firmly held at the edges, and glazing beads are recommended for all installations. Wider rebates as recommended for doors are also essential.

Plastics for glazing can be cut with metal-working or wood-working tools. Plastics glazing can be easily and quietly removed by using heat, and for this reason may sometimes be considered a security risk.

(iii) *Plastics window frames*

Window frames can be manufactured from extruded pigmented unplasticised PVC sections, cut and jointed by adhesives, welding, screwing

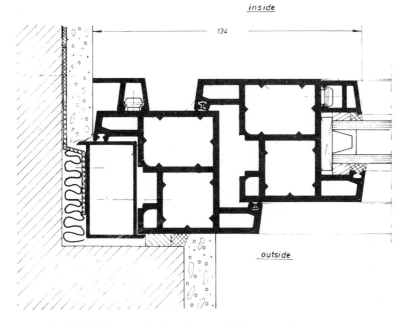

Fig. 4/25 Hollow profiled unplasticised PVC window frame (section).

or any combination of these methods. A section through a typical window-frame is depicted in Fig. 4/25, and a horizontal sliding window made from extruded unplasticised PVC sections in Fig. 4/26.

Fabrication, as well as being effected by the jointing of extruded sections, can also be carried out by injection moulding processes provided that enough units are required to make such processes economic.

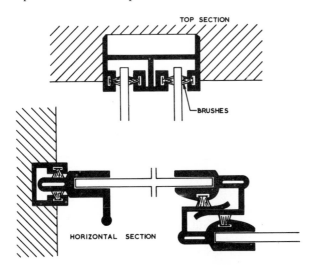

Fig. 4/26 Sections through horizontal sliding window frames of extruded unplasticised PVC.

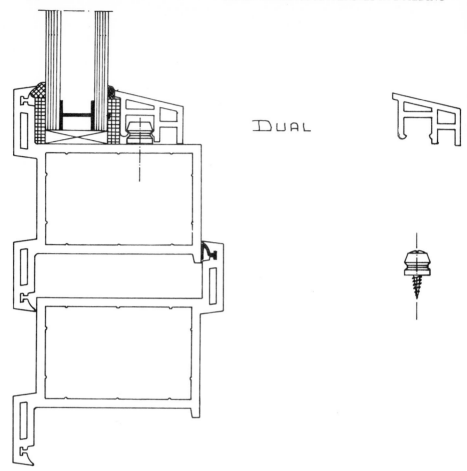

Fig. 4/27 Section through extruded rigid PVC window frame with double glazing.

Another type of extruded rigid PVC window frame is indicated in Fig. 4/27; double-glazing is included in the top part of the frame, the screws with clip heads and the loose beads for glazing being shown separately. Glass-reinforced plastics are also used for window frames of this type.

(iv) *Metal and wood frames with plastics covering*

Glass-reinforced plastics are sometimes used as coverings to preservative-impregnated wood or metal cores; PVC is also used to coat window frames of this type, the core being inserted into a preformed PVC section; alternatively the PVC may be applied as liquid to a fabricated wooden frame. If extruded PVC sections are used, the joints in the plastics extrusions must be sealed, in addition to jointing the metal or wooden frame.

A typical wooden window frame with a bottom hung sash made from plastics coated wood is depicted in Fig. 4/28, and a typical PVC and metal bar frame type of window in Fig. 4/29.

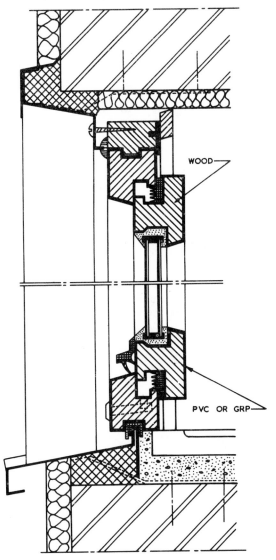

WOOD

PVC OR GRP

Fig. 4/28 Wooden window frame (section) with bottom hung sash from plastics coated wood.

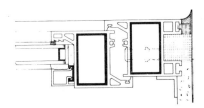

Fig. 4/29 Section through (jamb detail) PVC metal box type of window frame.

(v) *Gaskets and sealing strips*

Extrusions of butyl rubber, neoprene and polypropylene instead of putty, may be used for sealing, especially for steel or aluminium frames. Fig. 4/30

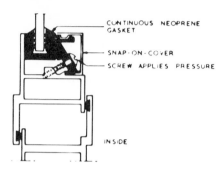

Fig. 4/30 Neoprene sealing gasket (section) for steel or aluminium window frame –
gasket seals by screw pressure.

shows a typical neoprene gasket that relies upon screws to apply pressure to the gasket to make an effective seal. The screws are hidden by continuous lengths of a metal snap-on cover finished to match the frame.

A type of gasket, made in two separate pieces, one bonded to the frame, and the other to the bead is shown in Fig. 4/31. A further type indicated in Fig. 4/32 has been successfully used for many years in the motor industry

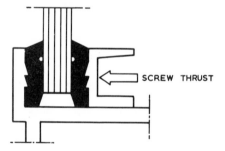

Fig. 4/31 Plastics sealing two-piece gasket – one bonded to frame, other to the bead.

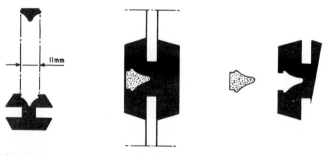

Fig. 4/32 Gaskets (sections), neoprene or butyl rubber, sealing by bead pressure.

and is now being used for jointing two sheets of glazing material, or glazing material to a metal frame. The gasket consists of a neoprene or butyl rubber strip shaped so that the insertion of the bead brings pressure to bear on the panels to ensure an effective seal.

For tall buildings the bead of the gasket shown in Fig. 4/32 should be fitted on the inside, both for reasons of security and ease of repair. There are certain advantages in rounding corners to reduce the number of joints and to avoid difficulties resulting from cutting and the fitting of mitres in gaskets.

(vi) *Accessories*

A wide selection of extruded sections is now available for draught excluders, sealing and jointing strips and other applications. Nylon, acetal and polyethelene are also being used increasingly to make hinges, window fasteners, casement stays and other window accessories.

When designing windows from PVC and glass-reinforced plastics, special care should be taken to ensure that the sections are properly reinforced at attachments to hinges and locks. Furthermore it should be remembered that many of the advantages of using plastics materials for windows can be lost if corrodible screws and fittings are used. Nylon coated metal hinges are available and may to some extent eventually overcome the present integral weakness in plastics window frames of the hinged opening types.

SECTION FIVE

CEILINGS

(a) Definitions

For the purpose of this handbook, the following definitions apply:—

1. *Ceiling:* A construction covering the underside of a floor or roof to provide the overhead surface of a room or other enclosed space.
2. *Suspended: Ceiling:* A ceiling hung at a distance from the floor or roof above.

(b) Ceilings (General)

Boards, tiles and panels are fixed as liners to the underside of floors and roofs to provide structure concealment and decorative finishes. The material selected may also provide some thermal and acoustic insulation. Fixing is usually by timber battens or steel suspension systems secured direct to structural elements at floor or roof levels, i.e. timberwork, concrete, steelwork etc. If a satisfactory level surface is available, lightweight tiles in a material such as expanded poly-styrene, may be bonded to the main ceiling (See Section Ten for information on suitable adhesives).

(c) Ceiling Materials (see also sub-section (e))

The selection of materials for normal ceilings will be influenced by factors such as appearance, ease of fixing, installation and maintenance costs, environ-mental and occupational conditions, flame spread and fire resistance character-istics as well as by requirements of the Building Regulations, etc. Plastics materials available for ceiling work include:—

1. *Expanded polystyrene*

Expanded polystyrene may be in the form of board, sheet, tile and roll, having plain, patterned or perforated appearance. The natural white surface provides a good self-finish, but the material can be decorated with paint or paper or keyed for direct plaster application. Decoration should be only by matt finish emulsion or flame-retardant paint since a gloss paint film increases flame spread. Self-extinguishing grades are available however, but as the materials used are often only part of a composite construction, it is difficult to provide specific flame-spread and fire-resistance data. Expanded polystyrene foam is employed as core material in sandwich panels.

2. *Polyurethane foam*

Polyurethane foam is available in slab and board form. Polyurethane may be obtained with outer facings of thin board or paper having self finishes. Alternatively, paint or plaster may be applied to these facings. Polyethylene is also used as a facing; it provides a vapour barrier and a surface that is easily cleaned. Polyurethane foam is also suitable for core material in sandwich panels. It can also be obtained ready bonded to plasterboard or other forms of rigid board, including sheet metal.

3. *PVC film-coated materials*

Glass-wool, plasterboard (and similar substrata), cane and mineral-fibre tiles can all be obtained PVC coated. The film provides an easily cleaned surface and the materials may be factory or site decorated.

(d) Suspended ceilings

Suspended ceilings, comprising boards, panels or tiles carried on grids of main and secondary members are used extensively, particularly over the large unobstructed areas provided by current building techniques. These ceilings fulfil the legitimate aesthetic function of structure and service concealment and may also provide:—

1. *Illumination*

Lighting fittings (luminaires) may be incorporated in a ceiling grid; alternatively, they may be suspended above a ceiling of translucent material, the resultant lighting being evenly diffused, as indicated in Figs. 5/1 and 5/2.

2. *Heating*

Certain forms of heating may be installed, but specialist advice should be sought on the types that are suitable for use with a plastics material ceiling.

3. *Ventilation*

The space above a suspended ceiling may be used as a plenum chamber, air being transferred to the room through grilles in the ceiling or through slotted or perforated tiles. Alternatively, the ceiling space may be used to house ventilation or air conditioning ductwork, etc.

4. *Thermal insulation*

The selected ceiling system because of its thermal properties may contribute to the total thermal resistance of a roof or floor.

5. *Acoustic correction*

The ceiling may be used for sound absorption purposes. It should be borne in mind that abnormal air currents are often produced in a ceiling incorporating services and these can create cleaning and maintenance problems, as well as fire risks.

Fig. 5/1 Translucent plastics ceiling panel (with lighting concealed above).

Fig. 5/2 Translucent plastics ceiling panel (c.f. Fig. 5/1).

(e) Materials for Suspended Ceilings (see also sub-section (c))

The selection of material for a suspended ceiling will likewise be influenced by the factors similar to those mentioned in sub-section (c) for "ceilings", i.e. by appearance, ease of fixing, installation and maintenance costs, environmental and occupational conditions, flame-spread and fire resistance charactertistics, accessibility, as well as by the requirements of the Building Regulations and special considerations such as illumination, acoustic correction etc. Optimum sizing should be assessed on points such as weight (and very lightweight plastics are available) and the liability of the material to sag in handling and fixing. The ease with which certain ceiling tiles may be cleaned or redecorated should also be taken into account when considering maintenance costs. Redecoration however can affect the acoustic properties of some materials.

Tiles, panels and sheets suitable for suspended ceilings are available in a range of plastics materials including polystyrene, polyurethane, PVC and acrylic. Tiles in wood, cane and mineral fibre and glass wool with vinyl coatings can also be supplied. The available materials may be broadly grouped under the following headings, though in general those listed under sub-section (c) have applications in suspended ceiling work: —

1. *Polystyrene*

Polystyrene tiles and panels including louvred and diffusion types are manufactured in a range of sizes for use with metal (or other forms) of suspension. Plain, moulded, coloured, perforated and corrugated patterns are available. Polystyrene provides a translucent material suitable for luminous ceilings or for providing luminous areas below light sources within conventional suspended ceilings.

2. *Expanded polyurethane*

This material is available covered with thin board or paper and having self-finishes. Alternatively, such facings may be painted. Polyethylene is also used as a facing, providing a vapour barrier and a surface that is easily cleaned. Polyurethane ready-bonded to plasterboard, as well as to other forms of rigid material, including sheet metal may also be obtained.

3. *PVC film*

Translucent or transparent PVC film is most frequently used where light diffusion or illumination is required. It can be applied in stretched form to give large areas of unobstructed ceiling, and also be used in single or double membrane form as a covering to panels or diffusion pans. PVC films are also applied to tiles made from glass wool, plasterboard, wood cane and mineral fibre. The resultant skins, which may be patterned and coloured, provide surfaces which are also easily cleaned.

4. *PVC and acrylic lamination*

Perforated sheet consisting of an inner skin of PVC with outer coverings of acrylic, may be obtained in the form of heat-laminated panel. High-impact strength, together with good thermal, acoustic, and light transmission properties are claimed for this product.

5. *Rigid PVC*

Tiles and panels, including louvred, corrugated, perforated and diffusion types are manufactured in colourless, white, and coloured PVC. They provide ceilings with good light transmission and are also easy to clean.

Rigid PVC is also used in strip form. These strips, sometimes stiffened with galvanised steel coring may be perforated or laid with gaps between. The resultant ceiling may be used for ventilation extraction purposes; if overlaid with material such as glass fibre, they can also provide considerable acoustic absorption.

6. *Acrylic*

Tiles and diffusers are produced in these materials.

SECTION SIX

PARTITIONS

(a) Introduction

Partitions are walls whose primary function is to divide space within a building or structure. They may be either load bearing or non-load-bearing. Structural load-bearing walls currently involve materials outside the scope of this Handbook, so only their facing and insulation aspects are considered here.

Non-load bearing partitions fall broadly into three categories:—

1. Permanent partitions
2. Demountable partitions
3. Sliding and folding partitions

(b) Selection of Partitions — Factors Involved

The following factors should be considered in selecting a partition:—

1. *Demountability*

The demolition or taking down of wet-construction walls involves the production of non-recoverable materials, damage to surrounding finishes as well as dirt and problems arising from concealed services. The ease with which demountable partitioning may be taken down varies from system to system and an ideal re-use is often difficult to find. Greater ease of taking down often means that the units have lower acoustic insulation qualities.

2. *Acoustic insulation*

Because of their mass, wet construction partitions (as compared with "dry") are more resistant to sound transmission. The performance of dry constructions is improved by double walling and by double glazing where appropriate, but these improvements increase cost and the parts are less easy to dismantle.

Where noise is likely to be an important factor, reference should be made to EEUA Handbook No. 25 (Measurement and Control of Noise). Additional construction costs may well be acceptable at the design stage since subsequent acoustic correction to provide satisfactory working conditions may prove expensive.

3. *Provision of services*

A permanent purpose-made partition can more readily accommodate services and service outlets than a demountable partition, but modification works thereto are difficult and dirty. Demountable partitions usually have limited facilities for running electric and telephone cabling in pilasters and skirtings, etc. The introduction of additional piped services could

involve the production of purpose-made walls which would cost more
and be difficult to take down.

4. *Fire resistance*

Wet-construction partitions can normally be expected to provide greater
fire resistance than demountable types. Surface spread of flame, in relation
to wall and ceiling linings, is a function of the surface material. In selecting
a suitable material the requirements of the current Building Regulations
should be borne in mind.

5. *Cost*

Demountable partitioning, though easy to take down and possessing
good acoustic insulation properties, is generally dearer than wet-construction walling, but it involves no wet trades or mess. Characteristics
such as flexibility, speed of erection and the possibility of re-use may
however influence the selection of a system.

(c) Permanent Partitions

Permanent partitions may be of brick and block or of dry construction as
described in the following sub-sections:--

(i) *Brick and block partitions*

1. *Wet-construction walls*

Wet-construction walls are made of brick or building block, fair-faced
or plaster coated. Sprayed, brush or flexible sheet material finishes are
usually applied to the walling, although fair-faced work may be left un-
decorated. Alternatively, certain of the boards or panels described elsewhere in this section may be fixed to the brick- or blockwork.

Lightweight concrete in situ or precast units containing expanded
polystyrene aggregate provide ultra lightweight walling units with excellent
thermal insulation properties. Nylon discs are available for locking
specially-grooved expanded concrete blocks together, and epoxy, polyester
and PVC mortar admixtures can be utilised to increase the strength and
durability of mortar mixes for brick and blockwork.

2. *Spray- and brush-applied surfaces*

Spray- and brush-applied PVC and epoxy resin-based compounds can
provide impervious wall finishes that are particularly functional in
laboratories, food and pharmaceutical factories, etc. These compounds
may be applied to a range of surfaces, being especially useful in conjunction
with porous insulation materials, thereby reducing the risk of interstitial
condensation. They can be employed to cover cracks and joints in walling
and though they provide good adhesion, they cannot be expected to deal
with subsequent movements.

Many of these plastics compounds can give rise to toxicity and fire hazards
while being applied. Working areas should therefore be well ventilated and the

operators properly protected. These necessary precautions may sometimes inhibit progress in adjoining areas, with possible effects on the programming of a project.

3. *Flexible sheet materials*

Flexible sheet materials, such as PVC surfaced walling covers, are applied to plastered coatings and also to certain smooth finishes, e.g. plasterboard, building boards etc. PVC sheet, with or without a backing of paper or fabric, is available in flat, quilted and padded forms, being sometimes provided with foam interlining. For use in dust-free zones in factories, a sterile and jointless wall covering may be obtained in a grade of PVC akin to vinyl flooring. This requires specialist fixing and involves the use of welded joints.

Self adhesive forms of PVC surfacings are also available, but for all applications, the manufacturer's instructions regarding preparation of surfaces and fixing should be carefully followed.

Expanded polystyrene in roll form is used for lining walls before applying the finishing surface; it provides an insulating membrane that reduces condensation.

(ii) *Dry-construction partitions*

Timber or metal studding is clad with boards or panels, self-tapping screws being used to fix claddings to metal frameworks. The claddings may be of plasterboard, strawboard, chipboard, asbestos metal or other conventional material, which in turn may be finished in the spray, brush or flexible sheet materials previously referred to in "1. Wet-construction walls". Alternatively the use of certain of the boards and panels listed below under sub-section (d) "Demountable Partitions" may be considered.

(d) Demountable Partitions — Materials Used

Demountable partitioning systems consist basically of a timber or metal framework which may be clad in a wide range of materials. The cladding incorporates doors and glazing and may be single or double-skinned and double-glazed. Partitions usually extend from floor to ceiling, but can be "low-height" types (fixed and free standing). Portable acoustic screens are also available, usually curved in plan. Partitioning for water closets and changing rooms is being increasingly used.

Partitions are often used with suspended ceilings but the compatibility of the two elements deserves careful thought before final selection is made. Furthermore, systems should be thoroughly investigated to ascertain in detail, their thermal/acoustic insulation and fire-resistance characteristics, particularly as these factors could influence Local Authority acceptance of a selected system (and, more important, its cladding).

Conventional boards and panels for cladding purposes may be finished in the spray, brush and sheet materials already referred to.

For demountable partitioning work itself, plastics materials are used in various forms as indicated below: —

1. *Panels*

These may be made from rigid foam cores of expanded polystyrene, polyurethane foam, expanded PVC, phenolic foam and phenolic/paper honeycombs. These materials form lightweight panels which are faced in metal, asbestos, plywood, hardboard etc. The panels have high strength/weight ratio and provide excellent thermal insulation. Doors having cores of expanded polystyrene can also be obtained.

2. *PVC sheeting*

PVC sheet can be applied to claddings of metal, hardboard, chipboard, plasterboard, asbestos, etc. Quilted and padded PVC is also obtainable.

3. *Laminated sheets*

Melamine formaldehyde laminated sheet is also used as a facing to chipboard, hardboard etc.

4. *Tiles*

PVC and polystyrene tiles require nailing or bonding to a backing material.

5. *Glazing materials*

PVC, acrylic, glass-reinforced plastics and PVC/acrylic are used as cladding or as glazing materials. Sheets of these materials transmit a high percentage of light and can be obtained in a large range of sizes and profiles.

(e) Sliding and Folding Partitions

These partitions are difficult to classify as walls or doors, but they fulfil in some measure the functions of both. They permit the division of large areas for multi-purpose use, though such subdivision may involve noise transmission problems.

These partitions are of timber or steel-rod frame construction: timber types consist of a series of independent panels of required ceiling height. They may be faced with melamine formaldehyde, and hinged so as to permit sliding and folding on ceiling or floor tracks. Hinges (sometimes of full length) may be of nylon or polypropylene; nylon is also used for track runners.

Steel-rod framed partitions of the collapsible type operated from a suspended track are vinyl covered and may incorporate an acoustic blanket interlining.

Sliding doors in acrylic are available for glazing use in conventional room dividers. Movable wall systems have recently been introduced into the United Kingdom; they incorporate plastics finishes and accessories.

SECTION SEVEN

FLOORING

(a) Introduction

Flooring tiles using thermoplastic resins were introduced into the United Kingdom in 1947. These inexpensive tiles (sometimes known as "Asphalt" tiles) are extensively used. Other forms incorporating polyvinyl chloride resin are available as tiles or sheet in wider colour ranges, and have added properties of toughness and flexibility.

The advent of these flooring materials has provided the architect and builder with an inexpensive flooring material that is easy to lay and maintain, and gives a hardwearing finish under a wide range of domestic, commercial and industrial applications, (always provided that the Building Regulations and the manufacturers' recommendations are adhered to). This proviso is particularly relevant when laying to timber sub-floors and to floors in contact with the ground (which latter application generally involves the use of a damp-resisting membrane).

The satisfactory appearance of a tiled floor depends largely on the smoothness and cleanliness of the screed on which the tiles are laid. Proprietary brands of smoothing compounds, very thinly applied, are available for improving slightly rough sand and cement screeds or for overlaying existing terrazzo or quarry tiling, etc.

Screeds based on synthetic anhydrite are also available. These are binders of the gypsum family made from a by-product of hydrofluoric acid and should not be confused with natural anhydrite. A number of advantages are claimed for them, including a faster rate of drying out when compared thickness for thickness with sand/cement screeds, and their suitability for use with sound reduction insulation and underfloor heating elements. Alternatively asphalt may be used; this constitutes a damp-proof course to new or existing floors and ensures that no moisture is trapped between floor and tile.

In the context of this section the names applied to the various types of tiles, e.g. "thermoplastic", "vinyl asbestos", etc., are those in common usage in the construction industry.

(b) Thermoplastic Tiles

Thermoplastic flooring tiles (sometimes known as "Asphalt" tiles) are made from a blended composition of mineral asphalt thermoplastic resins or from the solid or semi-solid products of coal or oil distillation, together with asbestos fibres and inert filler materials or pigments. They are described in B.S. 2592 (Thermoplastic Flooring Tiles) which specifies dimensions (229-mm × 229-mm × 5-mm or 3-mm) deflection, resistance to impact, indentation and curling. The 3-mm tile weighs about 6 kg/m^2.

67

(i) *Tile sizes*

Tiles are made in a range of plain and marbled colours which tend to be
dull. A wider range, where resinous binders are used in manufacture, can
be obtained however. Extras available include die-cut inserts, border strips in
widths from 25-mm to 152-mm, and coved skirtings 76-mm and 102-mm
high; the last two items are available only in limited colours.

(ii) *Methods of laying tiles*

The tiles are generally laid on sand and cement screeded (or other
specialist screeded) solid floors and bonded to them with manufacturer's
approved adhesive. Care should be taken to ensure that the sub-floor is
sound and well laid, that screeds are smooth and free from dust and dirt, and
that asphalt tiles are properly warmed before being bonded to sub-floors.

Whilst the tiles do not themselves form a damp-proof membrane, they
are generally unaffected by reasonable quantities of rising dampness and do,
in fact, "breathe". Consequently, the use of a continuous damp-proof membrane over concrete sub-floors is not essential unless a site is unduly wet. The
builder, contractor and others concerned should however, assess their responsi-
bility in view of Regulation C3 of the Building Regulations. Under-floor
heating can be satisfactorily incorporated in sub-floors, but the recommendations of British Standard Code of Practice 203 (Sheet and Tile Flooring—Cork,
Linoleum, Plastics and Rubber), should be observed in regard to maximum
permitted surface temperatures.

Tiles may also be laid over timber floors, but these should be properly
ventilated; an intermediate screed should also be used, preferably of hard
asphalt, since other forms are not consistently satisfactory.

(iii) *Selection factors*

It is advisable to seek expert advice before using asphalt tiles in association
with electrical equipment or in areas where static electricity might build up
(as in some industrial applications, and operating theatres) or where materials
handled involve explosive hazards. For thermal conductivity, a k value of
$0.432-0.504$ W/m$^\circ$C may be used.

Thermoplastic tiles are suitable for some commercial and domestic
applications (excluding kitchens). They are inexpensive to lay, serviceable,
hardwearing and fairly easy to maintain, but somewhat lacking in resilience
and are noisy and susceptible to indentation. They are reasonably resistant to
water, dilute acid and alkalis, but are softened by oils, greases and solvents,
though a special type is available that provides greater resistance to the three
last. This is achieved by the addition of a vinyl compound to the mix: it also
provides greater resistance to dirt, ingraining and surface staining. These tiles
however are somewhat susceptible to burns arising from cigarette stubbing.

(c) Vinyl Asbestos Tiles

Vinyl asbestos tiles are made from a blended composition of PVC binder,
asbestos fibre, fillers and pigments. The binder should consist substantially of
vinyl chloride polymer and/or copolymers, compounded with suitable plasticisers

and stabilizers. They are described in B.S. 3260, PVC (Vinyl) Asbestos Floor
Tiles, which specifies sampling methods, indentation, residual indentation,
deflection, impact, and indicates resistance to various substances.

(i) *Tile sizes*

Vinyl asbestos tiles are available in the following dimensions (mm) and
weights:—

Size (mm)	Thickness (mm)	Weight (kg/m²) (approx)
229 x 229	2.0	3.8
	2.5	5.1
	3.2	6.3
305 x 305	2.0	3.8
	2.5	5.1
	3.2	6.3

A range of plain and marbled colours and other surface effects are
available, the colours being brighter than those of the thermoplastic types
described in (b) above. Extras include die cut inserts, border strips from
13-mm to 152-mm wide, and coved skirting 76-mm and 102-mm high, these
last two items being available only in a limited range of colours.

(iii) *Method of laying tiles*

Vinyl asbestos tiles, like the "Asphalt" tiles just referred to in sub-section
(b), are also generally laid on sand and cement-screeded (or other specialist
screeded) solid floors to which they are bonded with manufacturer's approved
adhesive. The remarks and precautions indicated in sub-section (b) (ii) are in
fact equally applicable to the laying of vinyl asbestos tiles.

(iii) *Selection factors*

As with thermoplastic tiles, expert advice should be sought before using
vinyl asbestos tiles in conjunction with electrical equipment, or in areas where
static electricity could build up (as in some industrial applications and
operating theatres) or where materials handled involve explosive hazards. For
thermal conductivity, a k value of 0.432 to 0.504 W/m°C may also be used.

Vinyl asbestos tiles are suitable for domestic, commercial and industrial
uses. They are reasonably priced, hardwearing, resistant to indentation, water,
dilute acids, alkalis and greases, but are susceptible to attack by more powerful
solvents. They do not support combustion or assist flame spread, and they
resist cigarette burns.

(d) Flexible Polyvinyl Chloride Tiles and Sheets

Polyvinyl chloride tiles and sheets are made from a blended composition of
PVC binder, fillers and pigments. The binder should consist substantially of
vinyl chloride polymer and/or copolymers, compounded with suitable plasticisers

and stabilizers. They are described in B.S. 3261, (Flexible PVC Flooring), which like B.S. 3620 also specifies sampling methods, indentation, residual indentation, dimensional stability, deflection, impact and indicates resistance to various substances etc.

(i) *Sizes*

This type of tile is available in the following dimensions and weights, sheet also being obtainable as indicated below: —

Size (mm)	Thickness (mm)	Weight (kg/m²) (approx)
229 x 229	1.6 2.0 2.5	3.2 4.1 5.1
305 x 305	1.6 2.0 2.5	3.2 4.1 5.1
Sheet — in widths from 915-mm to 1830-mm.		

A range of plain and marbled colours is made. Extras include die-cut inserts, border strips in widths from 25-mm to 102-mm, as well as coved skirtings 76-mm and 102-mm high. The last two items are available only in a limited range of colours.

(ii) *Methods of laying*

These tiles like those of "Asphalt" and of vinyl asbestos are generally laid on sand and cement screeded (or other specialist screeded) solid floors, being bonded to them with manufacturer's approved adhesive. Care must again be taken to ensure that the sub-floor is sound and well laid, and that screeds are smooth and clear of dust and dirt. In this case however a continuous damp-proof membrane *must* be used, consisting (inter alia) of asphalt, hot-applied bitumen or bitumen felt bonded in hot-applied bitumen. Asphalt may be employed in place of a screed, but the other types mentioned should be installed as sandwich membranes between the structural slab and the screed. The tiles can also be satisfactorily laid direct to timber boarding, given a smooth and close jointed sub-floor. If this is uneven, a resin-bonded plywood or hardboard underlay or other forms of screed should be used in order to avoid the joint pattern being revealed, and to prevent premature wear.

(iii) *Selection factors*

Under-floor heating can be incorporated in sub-floors, but the recommendations of British Standard Code of Practice 203 (Sheet and Tile Flooring Cork, Linoleum, Plastics and Rubber) should also be followed in respect of maximum permitted surface temperatures. Special "anti-static" grades of flexible PVC flooring are available, but expert advice should be sought if an electrical problem of this kind arises, or if the flooring material may be used in conjunction with electrical equipment. For thermal conductivity purposes, k values ranging from 0.288 to 0.360 W/m°C may be used.

PVC tiles and sheet are suitable for domestic, commercial and industrial use. They are hardwearing but more expensive than other types; they are however reasonably soft to the tread, lighter in colour, resilient and resistant to indentation, dilute acids and alkalis, solvents, oils and greases. Their resistance to soiling is only moderate, and they are susceptible to cigarette burns; they can however be produced in forms which do not support combustion or assist flame spread.

(e) Other Methods of Using PVC in Flooring Materials

(i) *Backing materials*

Because of its toughness and resilience, PVC sheet is now extensively applied to PVC foam, needle felt, hessian and other backings which make a finished flooring both softer to the tread and quieter. In these forms they are available in a wide range of colours. Other backings used include synthetic rubberised felt, cellular rubber and vinyl sheeting.

These backed floorings can generally be laid to concrete, hardboard, plyboard or other forms of sub-floor. The manufacturer's advice should be sought on the question of damp courses, and the requirements of the Building Regulations adhered to. The backing material cannot be expected to take out sub-floor irregularities; good, even screeds are essential..

(ii) *Flooring finishes*

Chips or granules of coloured PVC are bonded in pure transparent plasticised PVC to give a marbled effect. The heavy gauge floor tiles and sheet so finished provide hard wearing and attractive looking surfaces. Another finishing method uses photography to reproduce marbles, woods, stones, woven materials, etc., on PVC film bases which are then coated with wearing surfaces of clear PVC. Manufacturer's fixing instructions must be strictly followed.

(iii) *PVC sheet*

Clear PVC sheet is used as a wearing skin to flooring materials such as cork or linoleum to improve their resistance to wear.

(iv) *Flexible vinyl sheet*

A form of flexible vinyl sheet flooring is built up from a clear film of PVC laminated to a layer of PVC compound. The back of the clear sheet is printed in a wide range of patterns. At present this sheeting material is used almost entirely for domestic applications since the film thickness is only about 0.1-mm.

(v) *Patterned vinyl*

Vinyl flooring is available with ribbed and diamond tread patterns, and may also be obtained with an aluminium oxide abrasive grain. Abrasive surfaces though "non-slip" may tend to become dirty.

(f) Carpeting

Synthetic fibres such as nylon, polyacrylonitril and polypropylene, are used alone or as blend with wool or acetate fibres to produce woven and tufted carpets or needleloam felts. PVC acrylic emulsions and synthetic rubber latices are used as bonding agents and as integral foam backings.

Woven carpet backings made from polypropylene fibrillated yarns are being increasingly used because of their light weight, durability, and competitive costs.

In a recent development of tufted carpets and felts, they are filled with various resins so that the tufts remain vertical. The resins now used include acrylic styrene, butadiene, vinyl or mixture resins; others are being investigated. The resin content increases carpet weight but is claimed to improve durability and increase resistance to crushing and deformation, thus making the carpet suitable for heavy foot traffic and light trucking.

(g) Jointless Flooring

Problems which may arise when tiles are used under certain conditions (for example in wet or damp) can be ameliorated by the use of welded plastic sheet, which as a floor covering material can be continued up the wall to form an impervious skirting. It should be remembered however that not all PVC materials available in roll form can be welded.

(i) *Types of jointless flooring materials*

One type of jointless floor, trowel-applied, utilises epoxy, polyurethane or polyester resins, mixed with graded aggregates and curing agents to give internal or external floor coverings to prepared sub-floors from 3-mm to 6-mm thick. These coverings provide impermeable finishes with good adhesion but with varying resistance to chemicals, oils, wearing and weathering; they can be very quickly brought into operation. The resins are available in a range of single colours having non-slip or self-polishing finishes. Epoxy types resembling marble, terrazzo or granolithic concrete can also be obtained. By adding granules of raw polystyrene to cement floor screeds, followed by buffing, a reasonably priced terrazzo substitute can be produced.

(ii) *Applications*

Epoxy resin flooring compounds may be trowel applied or poured; in the latter case they are self levelling. Due to their adhesive properties they are often used for patching work. The use of the trowelled compound is recommended where resistance to heavy mechanical wear is required, but if the chemical resistance or decorative aspects of the flooring are more important, then the self-levelling types may be preferred. These should only be laid on sound dry concrete floors, free from contamination, a smooth flat surface being essential for poured work. The self-levelling type is more simply and cheaply applied, but its resistance to mechanical wear and its slip characteristics are inferior. Polyester finishes are also available and these (and the epoxies) may be formulated as paints for brush application to floors.

The resistance to chemicals of manufactured flooring compounds of the epoxy and polyester types depends largely on the amount and type of extender used in the formulation. Generally, epoxide compounds are less resistant to chemicals than polyester types.

Polyurethane lacquers may be applied to old and new wood, linoleum, cork, concrete, stone and vinyl floors to provide a wearing surface of gloss and eggshell finish that can be easily cleaned. Increasing use is being made of the technique whereby the cellular voids in wood are impregnated with polyurethane, thus improving wearing properties without affecting the colour, while eliminating moisture movement.

(h) Floating Floor Quilts

Boards of expanded polystyrene, polyurethane foam, phenolic resin foam and PVC foam are laid on structural slabs to form a resilient screed on which to lay floor screeds or dry finishes. These boards reduce noise transmission and also provide thermal insulation. Expanded polystyrene ready-bonded to hardboard, PVC vinyl tiles or patent floor finishes, are available to provide a dry floor finish with elimination of wet trades. An accurate slab surface is required for these applications.

SECTION EIGHT

SERVICES

(a) Introduction

Plastics are mainly used in building services as direct replacements of traditional materials. For example, there are water mains and rainwater goods in PVC, waste systems in polypropylene, as well as electric cables insulated and sheathed with a variety of polymers.

It should be remembered, however, that since plastics are very poor electrical conductors, PVC pipelines cannot be traced by electrical means; if such provision is required, copper tracer cables may be buried in the pipe tracks. For the same reason the contents of plastics pipe systems cannot be thawed by electrical techniques which use the pipes as conductors, though special electric heating tubes are available for this purpose.

The main service applications of plastics materials however are tabulated below against the general classifications indicated, and are described in the subsequent sub-sections (b) to (k): —

Classification (Application)	Service
Water and gas	Water mains and services Gas mains and services
Mechanical	"Vacuum" lines Instrument lines Ventilation equipment
Surface water and sewage disposal	Soil and waste water systems Rainwater systems Underground drainage
Electrical	Cables, conduit, skirting, lighting, earthing, etc.

(b) Water Mains and Services

(i) General

Water mains and water service pipe of plastics materials have been used for many years in the UK and in Europe. In the UK, unplasticised PVC is usually employed for water distribution and polythene pipe for water services from the mains to the house. More recently, unplasticised PVC pipe has been used for cold-water services in houses and industrial buildings.

(ii) Polyethylene water service pipe

Polyethylene is available as two distinct grades, namely low-density and high-density polyethylene. As indicated in Table 1/3, the nominal density of

the former is not greater than about 930 kg/m^3, and that of the latter is
not less than about 930 kg/m^3. As a result there are two standards for
polyethylene water pipe: BS 1972 (Polythene Pipe, Type 32, for Cold Water
Services) covers the low-density grades and specifies details of the compounds
used, the classification and dimensions of the pipe as well as test methods.
BS 3284 (Polythene Pipe, Type 50, for Cold Water Services) specifies similar
details for high-density polyethylene grades.

The associated standards, BS 1973 (Polythene Pipe, Type 32, for General
Purposes Including Chemical and Food Industry Uses) and BS 3796
(Polythene Pipe, Type 50, for General Purposes Including Chemical and Food
Industry Uses) cover the low and the high-density grades respectively for the
purposes indicated.

Cold water service pipe always contains carbon black to protect the
polymer from ultra violet light while in storage or in use, and to prevent the
growth of green algea in the water. For diameters up to 50-mm, it is available
in coiled lengths up to some 150 m and for diameters of over 50-mm, it may be
obtained in straight lengths up to 6 m.

Metal compression fittings are normally used throughout. Jointing
techniques are now well established and the joints give long, trouble-free
service. The ease of jointing, the flexibility of the pipe (which allows large
radius bends) coupled with its availability in long lengths, makes pipe installation easy, especially for temporary water supplies or for providing water to
out-buildings and fields. In addition, trenchless laying (mole ploughing)
methods can be employed where long lengths of underground installations
are required.

Polyethylene is unaffected by water, and by soils which corrode metals.

(iii) *Unplasticised PVC water pipe*

B.S. 3505 (Unplasticised PVC Pipe for Cold-Water Services) gives details of
the compounds used, and of the pressure rating and size of the pipe for carry-
ing potable water. The companion standard B.S. 3506 (Unplasticised PVC
Pipe for Industrial Purposes) describes general purpose unplasticised PVC pipe
for industrial use.

Unplasticised PVC pipe is available in sizes up to 610-mm (24-in) nominal
diameter in wall thicknesses suitable for pressures of 0.6, 0.9, 1.2 and 1.5
MN/m^2 (equivalent to 60, 90, 120 and 150-m head of water) at 20°C.
These pipes are normally supplied in lengths of up to 6-m but longer lengths
can be obtained against special orders. They are joined by mechanical joints
and fittings or by solvent welded joints. A wide range of fittings is available
to B.S. 4346 (Joints and Fittings for Use with Unplasticised PVC Pressure
Pipes).

Screwed joints may be used for sizes up to 76.2-mm (3-in) nominal diameter but the screw thread automatically derates the pipe (because the wall
thickness is reduced). It also introduces a hazard since the thread can act as a
notch and initiate a crack. Solvent-welded joints should be used for pipes
larger than 76.2 mm in above-ground installations. Mechanical rubber-ring
joints are generally used in underground installations since solvent welding is
impracticable. The small-diameter pipes for domestic cold-water systems are

jointed by solvent welding, adaptors being available for attachment to taps and valves.

Unplasticised PVC is completely unaffected by water and corrosive soils (c.f. polyethylene).

(iv) *Handling and storage*

Unplasticised PVC pipes are relatively light and easy to handle and this may lead to abuse in certain circumstances. Pipes should not be thrown or dropped, particularly when unloading. They should either be handed down or rolled via planks to the ground, which in turn must be clear of large or sharp stones. It is advisable to take extra care with unplasticised PVC pipe during cold weather.

For purposes of site storage, flat ground, free from objects such as large or sharp stones, should be used, and the pipes stacked up to six layers high with the sockets protruding at alternate ends. During long-term storage, in a merchant's premises for example, the pipes should be stacked in racks. Continuous support along the whole pipe length is ideal, but in any case, timbers of 75-mm bearing width, placed at a maximum of 1.5-m centres, should be used for supports. This permits stacking up to ten layers. Whenever possible it is better to store indoors and out of prolonged direct sunlight.

(c) Gas Mains and Services

(i) *General*

The use of plastics pipes and fittings in gas distribution systems may be divided into two categories. The first concerns the distribution of fuel gas (domestic), such as coal gas, converter gas or natural gas for heating; the second, the distribution of air or other permanent non-fuel gases for scientific or medical purposes.

(ii) *Fuel gases*

Until about 1965, plastics pipes and fittings for the distribution of fuel gases had been little used in the United Kingdom, because most of the gas produced by the Gas Boards had been derived from coal and contained high but variable amounts of aromatic solvents, such as benzene. These caused the plastics materials to swell and to lose strength. The increasing use of converted gas derived from oil and, more recently, natural gas has changed the situation because neither of these gases contain harmful amounts of aromatic solvents, and they can therefore be safely transported in plastics pipes.

The Gas Council in co-operation with the British Plastics Federation, has drawn up specifications for pipes of PVC and polyethylene for use with natural and towns gas containing not more than one per cent (by vol.) of aromatic hydrocarbons. These specifications (GC/PS/PL1 for PVC and GC/PS/PL2 for polyethylene pipe and fittings) cover gas pressures up to 4 bar (60 lbf/in^2), and form the basis for British Standards now (1972) in preparation. The external pipe sizes are from $\frac{3}{4}$ in. to 12 in. nominal in accordance with Table 1 of BS 3867 (Outside Diameters and Pressure Ratings of Pipe of Plastics Materials). Pipe lengths are 3, 6 and 9m for PVC and 6, 9 and 12m, for polyethylene, which in addition can be coiled in 50m lengths. The pipes have to be a canary yellow colour. Jointing is by solvent welding for PVC, and fusion welding for polyethylene, except where mechanical joints are needed to connect to pipes of a different material, e.g. to cast iron or steel.

The Gas Boards are using plastics pipes for distribution mains and underground service pipes, but not for services inside buildings.

(iii) *Distribution of non-fuel gases*

Permanent gases such as air, nitrogen, argon and oxygen at low pressures, are usually distributed in pipes made from acrylonitrile-butadiene-styrene (ABS), because this material is less brittle than unplasticised PVC pipe to B.S. 3506, although this is sometimes used. High-impact PVC as specified for fuel gas pipes can also be employed. Pipes of this material should preferably be solvent welded, but screwed connectors are available if required. Valves, stop-cocks and a variety of branch connectors are also available as well as transition pieces to metal accessories. Pipes should be provided with adequate support and allowance for expansion. A synthetic fibre reinforced plasticised PVC pipe can be employed as flexible tubing when this is required for connection to or from moving or vibrating equipement. This pipe is available in sizes up to 38-mm ($1\frac{1}{2}$-in) internal diameter, and has working pressures, depending on size, from 0.3 MN/m^2 to 1.4 MN/m^2.

(d) Vacuum Lines

(i) *General*

In building services, vacuum lines can be used for two purposes, i.e. to evacuate air or other gases or vapours from plants or rooms, and to remove solid matter by entrainment, e.g. vacuum cleaning and dust extraction.

(ii) *Materials and jointing*

Pipe to B.S. 3506 (Unplasticised PVC Pipe for Industrial Purposes), is suitable and competitive in price. It is easily installed, available in a wide range of sizes and can easily be hot bent to give smooth bends that provide little resistance to flow. It is also corrosion-resistant and has a smooth internal surface. Solvent cemented joints ensure freedom from leaks. In the extraction of vapours or vapour-laden air, the dew point of the vapour could be reached. Care should therefore be taken to ensure that there are no dead-ends or pockets in which condensed strong solvents can collect and attack the PVC (assuming that they would do so). If such traps cannot be avoided, they must be drainable.

(e) Instrument Lines

(i) *Materials*

Flexible polyethylene tubes are used for transmitting air over long distances in order to operate meters, controllers, pressure gauges and recorders, as well as for the remote measurement of liquid levels. Nylon and plasticised PVC is also used in some low-pressure applications.

(ii) *Jointing*

Plastics tubes can be obtained with the same dimensions as their steel or copper counterparts. Threaded joints with screwed fittings are not recommended. The preferred joint is made with a compression fitting specially designed for use with steel or copper tube. Multi-core tubes are also available. Compression fittings are more expensive than screwed joints, but enable joints to be broken down for cleaning and modification of the line.

(iii) *Advantages and disadvantages*

The rapidity of making the few joints required and the general ease of handling help to keep installation costs low. It should be remembered however that the flexibility, which is an advantage during installation, may necessitate line supports being spaced at closer intervals than normal in order to prevent condensate accumulating at points of greatest sag. In many cases, the tube lines may be run in ducts or on trays, in which case the question of extra support will not arise.

The corrosion resistance of polyethylene tube is a particular advantage. Internal corrosion of steel instrument lines is not normally serious in itself, but the development of rust and scale should be minimised since solid particles may reach instruments, etc. Many chemical plant atmospheres cause rapid external corrosion of steel instrument tubes with consequent high maintenance (and even replacement) costs. Though polyethylene tube does not corrode, it may deteriorate by exposure to certain oils, and strong solvents. It can also be damaged when work is proceeding on adjacent equipment or services. Runs of polyethylene tube should therefore be located so as to minimise this possibility, and to avoid proximity to hot surfaces; care should also be taken to avoid or minimise such hazards.

The advantage of flexibility in making easy the neat attachments possible is clearly indicated in Fig. 8/1 which shows polyethylene tubes in pneumatic instrument lines.

(f) Ventilation Equipment

(i) *General*

The need for mechanical ventilation increases each year as the advantages are appreciated of a properly controlled environment for both staff and equipment. In the past, plastics duct-work has been considered necessary only where aggressive conditions were likely to be met, but it has much to offer as general-purpose duct-work, and its use may be expected to grow quickly in this field. Plastics are also being used for other components of ventilation systems, e.g. fan casings, impeller blades, grilles and roof outlets (see fig. 8/2).

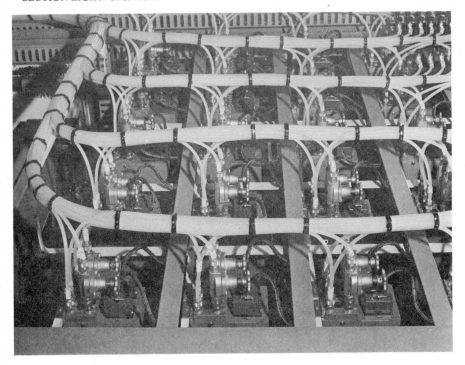

Fig. 8/1 Polyethylene tubes in pneumatic instrument lines.

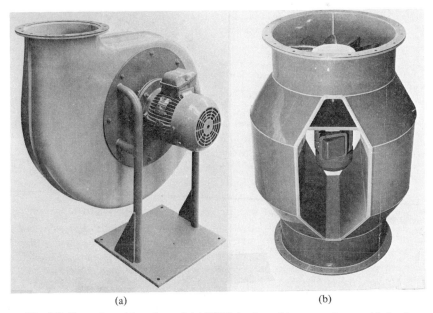

(a)   (b)

Fig. 8/2 Fan units, with casings of rigid PVC sheets, and incorporating moulded polypropylene impellers, (a) and (b).

Fig. 8/2(c) Fan casing and roof outlet made from glass-reinforced plastics.

(ii) *Advantages of plastics for duct-work*

These may be summarised as follows:

1. Excellent corrosion resistance
2. Good sound attenuation
3. Lightness
4. Simple fixing and ease of assembly (handling)
5. Low maintenance – decoration unnecessary.

(iii) *Materials available*

A. *Standard pipe*

A duct-work system has the same requirements as other pipe systems, i.e. cheap, light-weight and leak-proof tubes, as well as a simple jointing and fitting system needing little on-site work. Plastics pipe designed for other purposes is therefore suitable and any of the heavy tonnage plastics can be used. The one most readily available is rigid PVC to B.S. 3506 (Unplasticised PVC Pipe for Industrial Purposes), in nominal sizes up to 457-mm (18-in) diameter. A suitable pipe with constant wall thickness can be selected from the various classes of this range in sizes up to 305-mm (12-in) nominal. Table 8/1 is an abstract from the table of dimensions in B.S. 3506 for pipe approximately 3-mm ($\frac{1}{8}$-in) thick, this being considered the most suitable wall thickness for ventilation ducts. Branches can be welded to such pipe, and joints between pipe lengths can be made by spigot-and-socket, solvent cement, or by welding.

For pipe sizes between 305-mm (12-in) and 457-mm (18-in) nominal diameter, B.S. 3506 specifies increasing wall thicknesses, that at 18-in nominal being 4.9-mm (0.193-in) for example.

TABLE 8/1:   UNPLASTICISED PVC PIPE FOR INDUSTRIAL USES

(1)	(2)		(3)		(4)
	Pipe to B.S. 3506 with Wall Thickness of about 3—mm ($\frac{1}{8}$-in)				
Nominal Size in	*Average O.D.*		*Average Wall Thickness*		*Class*
	mm	*in*	*mm*	*in*	
2	60.4	(2.37)	3.1	(0.140)	4
3	89.0	(3.50)	3.1	(0.123)	2
4	114.0	(4.50)	3.6	(0.140)	3
6	168.3	(6.60)	3.2	(0.130)	1
8	219.0	(8.60)	3.2	(0.130)	1
10	273.0	(10.70)	3.2	(0.130)	1
12	324.0	(12.70)	3.2	(0.130)	1

B. *Special extrusions*

Manufacturers also offer a special ventilation series of pipe in unplasticised PVC. This has a similar specification to B.S. 3506, but is not yet covered by a British Standard. The main differences are that the unplasticised PVC pipe is offered in a wall thickness of 3.2-mm ($\frac{1}{8}$-in) for all diameters, and that these are given as internal diameters, specified in 25.4-mm (1-in) steps between 50-mm and 457-mm (2 and 18-in). Bends, branches and joints are made in a similar way to those of pipes to B.S. 3506. Rectangular extruded duct work in unplasticised PVC is available in sizes up to 305-mm (12-in) for the longer side. (See also EEUA Handbook No. 20: Thermoplastic Pipework and Ducting in Unplasticised PVC and Polythene).

C. *Other pipe systems*

There are a number of pipe systems in unplasticised PVC manufactured for other purposes, such as soil pipes and underground drainage pipes. These have a variety of fittings that are joined by solvent cementing or by rubber sealing rings. Such systems have wall thicknesses of approximately 3.5-mm (0.14-in) and are made in 75-mm, 100-mm and 150-mm (3-in, 4-in and 6-in) nominal sizes. They offer the cheapest form of ducting in their sizes since the pipes incorporate joint fittings which offer greater flexibility of design. (See Fig. 8/3). That Fig. also indicates a 17-storey block system which has been successfully installed with such pipes and fittings.

D. *Fabrication of ductwork from sheet*

The cost of an extruded duct in unplasticised PVC is less than for duct fabricated from sheet since unplasticised PVC sheet is already more expensive (per kg) than extruded standard pipe of the same thickness. There are however designs which demand unusual sizes or shapes of duct and these must therefore be fabricated from sheet.

Unplasticised PVC sheet suitable for the fabrication of ducting is available to B.S. 3757 (Rigid PVC Sheet). The pressed unplasticised PVC

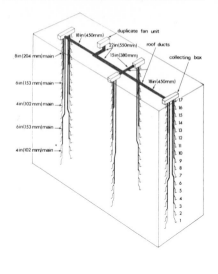

Fig. 8/3 Unplasticised PVC pipes with spigot and socket joints, and (right) application in
multistorey flats.

sheets (Type A2 in Part 1) and extruded unplasticised PVC sheets (Type C2
in Part 2) are particularly suitable, and are also much cheaper than the other
types of unplasticised PVC sheet covered by B.S. 3757. They are offered in
a grey colour which matches closely the grey of extruded unplasticised PVC
pipe.

Ducts are fabricated from these sheets by bending heated sheets along
a line to form rectangular ducts (or through a continuous curve to form
circular ducts), then welding the edges together along the length of the
duct. Sheets 3.2-mm ($\frac{1}{8}$-in) thick are recommended for this purpose. Ducts
over 457-mm (18-in) diameter usually need stiffeners, in the form of a framed
angle or PVC on edge, welded to the ducts.

E. *Other plastics materials used*

Other suitable plastics are polypropylene, and to a smaller extent, glass-
reinforced plastics. Polypropylene extruded pipe is available black or
colourless, in a range of sizes up to 305-mm (12-in), in accordance with the
the dimensions specified in B.S. 3867 (Dimensions of Pipe of Plastics
Materials). A comprehensive range of fittings is available for pipe sizes up
to 152-mm (6-in) diameter. Ducts larger than 305-mm (12-in) diameter or
of special shape, must be fabricated from polypropylene sheet.

Polypropylene ducts whether made from sheet or from extruded pipe
cost more than those from unplasticised PVC. Unless, therefore, the

special temperature resistance or corrosion resistance properties of polypropylene are required, unplasticised PVC is usually preferred, especially as this is self-extinguishing when exposed to fire.

PVC or polypropylene ductwork is often strengthened by means of an external laminate of glass-reinforced polyester (GRP). This ensures that large ducts are sufficiently rigid without employing large thicknesses of expensive thermoplastics; it also enables the duct to be used at higher termperatures than without the reinforcement, especially in the case of PVC ductwork (see (iv) below). An example of fabricated ducting made in polypropylene reinforced with glass reinforced plastics is illustrated in Fig. 8/4.

This type of ducting is always purpose-made and is generally less costly than metal ducting in corrosive environments. Furthermore, being rigid, it does not need closely-spaced supports, and, with the correct combination of materials can be made to resist many chemical liquids and fumes. Its smooth surface minimises resistance to flow and also inhibits the formation of internal coatings.

(iv) *Working temperatures*

Dimensional changes caused by temperature variations are much larger for plastics ducts than for metal, and due allowance for this should be made in design stages. Much of the thermal expansion or contraction can be accommodated by careful design and by the inherent flexibility of the plastics, but expansion joints are often necessary. Spigot-and-socket joints with rubber sealing rings can easily absorb expansions of about 20-mm ($\frac{3}{4}$-in) at each joint; or a sliding spigot-and-socket joint with a flexible shroud can be used. Polypropylene bellows can be employed where good chemical resistance is essential but are more expensive than spigot-and-socket joints.

The maximum temperatures at which these plastics materials will perform satisfactorily for long periods is about $50°C$ for unplasticised PVC and $90°C$ to $100°C$ for polypropylene. Unplasticised PVC should not be exposed for long periods to temperatures above $70°C$, unless reinforced by GRP. As indicated in E above, PVC or polypropylene ducts with GRP reinforcement may be used at higher temperatures; the upper limit is usually determined by the properties of the resin in the GRP and can be substantially higher than $100°C$.

(v) *Handling and fixing*

Unplasticised PVC duct-work (and other plastics duct-work) is much lighter than its metal equivalent, and can normally be lifted and unloaded by hand; it does not lend itself to mechanical handling. When transporting by road, care should be taken to prevent vibration from being transmitted to the ducting. Straw bolsters or other soft padding should be laid across the bed of the lorry. When ducting pipe is transported in layers, soft packing should be fitted between each layer. Hard narrow supports (timbers) should not be used, because they concentrate loads and vibration stress into small areas and can cause deformation or cracking.

The maximum distance between supports for unplasticised PVC ducting should be 2.4-m reducing to 1.5-m for duct-work above 810-mm (32-in) diameter.

Fig. 8/4 Fabricated plastics ducting (polypropylene with glass-reinforced plastics) for an industrial plant.

(vi) *Handling and storage*

The methods and precautions outlined for plastics service pipes in sub-section (b) (iv) on page 76 should also be adopted for plastics ductwork required for site storage or long-term storage.

(g) Soil and Waste-Water Systems (above ground)

(i) *General*

The changes in the design of soil and waste systems in recent years, especially in those for domestic installations, has been given added impetus by the design of plastics pipe systems, especially in unplasticised PVC. B.S. 4514 (Unplasticised PVC Soil and Ventilating Pipe, Fittings and Accessories), provides some guidance to users of these systems, and a B.S. for waste systems is being prepared. Unplasticised PVC soil systems are extensively used in new domestic installations.

For soil systems, only one plastics material is used, namely unplasticised PVC together with a small amount of its high temperature resistant variant PVC/chlorinated PVC.

For waste systems, plastics with higher temperature resistance are employed, there being four types in general use for domestic purposes: acrylonitrile-butadiene-stryrene (ABS), chlorinated PVC, polypropylene, or high-density polyethylene. For some industrial installations, factors other than temperature also arise, such as chemical resistance to solvents, acids, alkalis, etc. Because of the striking differences in the types of plastics used, the two systems are dealt with separately below, but for design purposes they may have to be considered together where soil and waste water are combined in a single system.

(ii) *Soil pipes (Unplasticised PVC)*

The advantages of unplasticised PVC as the material for soil pipe systems are:—

1. *Easy fixing*

Most joints are of the rubber-ring sealed spigot and socket type; to some extent these also act as expansion joints. Solvent cemented joints may be used; in which case some experience is needed by the installation personnel.

2. *Excellent corrosion resistance*

Unaffected by the weather or by sunlight, and offers a smooth unfouled inner surface throughout its life.

3. *Low cost*

Unplasticised PVC systems are more than 20 per cent cheaper than cast-iron ones (unplasticised PVC pipes and fittings are more expensive than those made from self-finished cement asbestos, but there are savings in ease of handling, labour and fixing).

4. *Lightness*

Unplasticised PVC systems weigh approximately only one-seventh as much as those of cast iron, and half those of cement asbestos.

5. *Minimum maintenance*

Painting is unnecessary (unless a change of colour is required), while the material is flexible enough to accommodate movements in the structure.

(iii) *Types of soil pipe systems*

B.S. 4514 specifies requirements for unplasticised PVC solid and ventilating pipe fittings and accessories for above-ground drainage systems intended to convey normal domestic effluents. Three systems, of nominal sizes 75-mm, 100-mm and 150-mm (3-in, 4-in and 6-in), are described, the available colours being black and grey. Unplasticised PVC soil and ventilating pipes have been available for several years, and a number of non-interchangeable systems have been developed. Only pipe and fittings designed for the chosen systems should therefore be bought – at least for the time being.

Unplasticised PVC soil systems are designed for the single-stack plumbing system; the fittings and accessories allow a flexible design. Where necessary, a separate venting system can be used and these are available in 50-mm and 75-mm (2-in and 3-in nominal) sizes. Unplasticised PVC pipe has adequate temperature resistance in domestic soil systems but pipe made from chlorinated PVC, polypropylene and ABS is recommended where large volume discharges of very hot water (90°C to 95°C) are possible. There is yet no British Standard which covers the use of these particular materials, but the provision of a complete soil and waste system as one system should be considered at the design stage.

(iv) *Fixing soil pipes*

Spigot-and-socket joints are used to join the pipe sections and fittings. These joints may be either rubber-ring sealed or solvent-cemented. Rubber-ring sealed joints are to be preferred, and are assembled with a special lubricant. They are designed to leave sufficient room for longitudinal movement of the pipe, especially that caused by expansion when hot water is discharged. The branch fittings and short connections carry bosses to take $1\frac{1}{4}$-in, $1\frac{1}{2}$-in and 2-in nominal connections for waste pipes. (See (v) Waste-pipe systems). An insert boss can also be fixed to any part of the system by simple solvent-cementing.

Vertical pipework is secured with plastics or plastics coated metal holder-bats spaced at 2-m intervals. For horizontal runs the brackets should be spaced at 900-mm intervals.

PVC soil systems may be used in conjunction with unplasticised PVC underground drainage pipes; connectors are also available for jointing all sizes of unplasticised PVC to cast iron, earthenware or pitch fibre drains. Connections to W.C. pans are made in many ways (see Fig. 8/5), such as by reversion or shrink joint, rubber-ring seal, or by flexible plastics conversion piece. No mastic is used with these, and a watertight flexible seal is easily obtained (even though mastic joints can be employed if required).

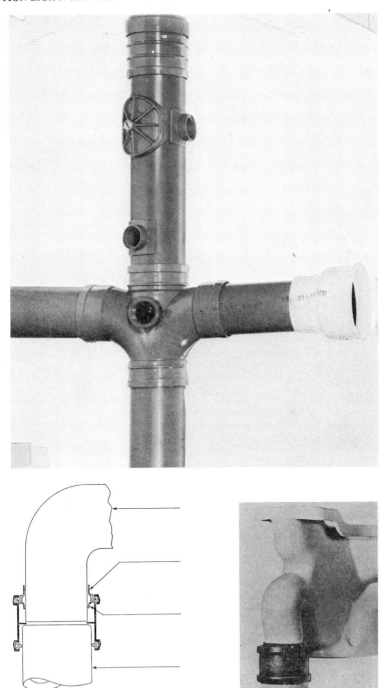

Fig. 8/5 Examples from plastics soil pipe systems.
        Top: Junction with fittings and connections.
        Bottom: Plastics pan adaptor.

Skilled labour should be used for fixing and jointing in all these methods, and reference made to "Guide to the Installation of Unplasticised PVC Soil-Pipe Systems", issued by The Institute of Plumbing Ref. No. X, 1970.

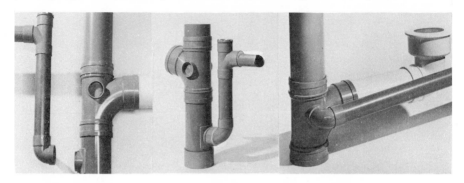

Fig. 8/6 Screwed connectors for waste-pipes.
Top (left and centre): Branch boss adaptor bends.
Top (right): Spigot boss.
Bottom: Self-locking screwed boss.

(v) *Waste-pipe systems*

Four different plastics are used for these systems, and all give the following advantages:—

1. *Easy fixing*

Rubber-ring sealed joints are suitable for all types of pipes, and solvent-cemented joints for PVC, ABS (see (vii) "Fixing" below) are used extensively. Some screwed connections are employed for fixing to appliances and traps — see Fig. 8/6.

2. *Excellent resistance to corrosion*

All the plastics used are unaffected by domestic aqueous effluent at the highest temperatures attainable. They are also generally resistant to acids and alkalis, e.g. in factories where there is a risk of chemicals passing through the waste system. A correct selection of the appropriate plastics material and joint sealing will also meet most of the conditions where organic solvents and oils are present in the effluent.

3. *Minimum maintenance*

No painting is required (unless a change of colour is required); moreover the likelihood of pipeline repairs due to damage by frost is small.

4. *Cost*

There is little to choose between the various plastics systems all of which cost about one third that of non-ferrous systems.

(vi) *Types of waste-pipe systems*

Waste water systems in acrylonitrile-butadiene-styrene (ABS), chlorinated PVC, polypropylene and high-density polyethylene are available in nominal sizes of $1\frac{1}{4}$-in, $1\frac{1}{2}$-in and 2-in diameter with accessories, traps and overflows to match. As there are four different plastics to choose from and as pipe sizes vary between systems using the same material, it is essential to use accessories designed for the system selected, since there is little or no interchangeability. The system is usually white but colours such as "coppertone" and "grey" are also offered.

A British Standard for waste pipes is being prepared. B.S. 3943 (Plastics Waste Traps), is one of the few for plastics components which is strictly a performance standard (no mention is made of materials). The awaited British Standard is expected to be a performance standard, complementary to B.S. 3943. Because of the present range of available sizes however, there is no certainty regarding preferred sizes.

In addition to the domestic waste systems described above, low-density polyethylene systems are available for industrial and laboratory waste pipes. These use socket-welded joints and a wide range of accessories and fittings. In laboratory installations care should be taken that solvents are not trapped where they can attack the polyethylene.

(vii) *Fixing of waste-pipe systems*

The pipe should be supported at not less than 900-mm intervals, and at least one expansion joint allowed for each 1.8-m length. Rubber-ring sealed joints where used, act as expansion joints, but a special expansion coupling is needed for solvent cement systems. Solvent-cement joints cannot be used with polypropylene or polyethylene, and coupling to the soil-pipe is usually by a rubber-ring joint. Any standard waste trap can be connected to the system by means of adaptors.

(h) Rainwater Systems

(i) *General*

Since 1960 the use of plastics in rainwater systems has grown remarkably, and over 90 per cent of all new installations for housing now use unplasticised PVC rainwater systems. These are compatible with the established half-round systems in cast iron, cement-asbestos and aluminium; renovation, using unplasticised PVC gutter and/or pipe work is easily effected. It is technically feasible to use other plastics, such as polyethylene for rainwater systems, but unplasticised PVC is the preferred material in the United Kingdom; the information in this handbook relates to systems made from it.

(ii) *Characteristics of unplasticised PVC rainwater systems*

The use of unplasticised PVC for rainwater systems brings the following advantages:—

1. *Easy fixing*

Once the gutter brackets and pipe supports are in place the rest snaps into position and no mastic or bolts are needed.

2. *Excellent resistance to corrosion*

The material is unaffected by the elements and by sunlight when properly compounded and pigmented.

3. *Low initial cost*

The systems are much cheaper than others having the same performance and decorative finish. Considerable savings may also be made because no maintenance is needed, e.g. the system needs no painting unless a change of colour is required.

4. *Lightness*

Because of the material's lightness, it is easily handled. A typical system weights half that of an aluminium, and a seventh that of a cast-iron system.

(iii) *Types of unplasticised PVC rainwater systems*

External unplasticised PVC rainwater systems are available in the plain half-round type in gutter sizes from 75-mm to 150-mm (3-in to 6-in) nominal with all necessary fittings and accessories. The gutters and pipes are available in the following lengths:—

Gutters		Pipes	
m	ft	m	ft
2	6	2	6
3	9	2.6	8
4	12	3.3	10
–	–	4	12
–	–	6	18

the systems themselves being made in a range of self colours, black, grey or white.

A limited range of systems in ogee and box-section gutters are available, the latter often with rectangular pipes. Combined fascia and gutter systems are also obtainable. Boundary wall, fascia and the various valley gutters are available in glass-reinforced plastics, but the need to satisfy the Building Regulations must be borne in mind.

Internal rainwater pipe in unplasticised PVC is offered as 75-mm (3-in) nominal pipe with sealed joints and accessories. Where pressure head requirements are specified, pipe to B.S. 3506 (Unplasticised PVC Pipe for Industrial Purposes) may be used as internal rainwater pipe. Part 1 of B.S. 4576 (Unplasticised PVC Rainwater Goods) specifies metric unit standards for half-round gutters and circular pipe. The available rainwater systems are not yet truly interchangeable, however, and this position is likely to continue for some years. Particular attention should therefore be paid to fittings and accessories especially when ordering for repair or expansion of premises; early signs of any standardisation in the design of new installations should be carefully observed.

Fig. 8/7 Plastics gutter-showing supports connections and bends (unplasticised PVC).

(iv) *Fixing and accessories* (see Fig. 8/7)

Supports for unplasticised PVC gutters should also have a maximum spacing of 900-mm; they should be fixed to a vertical fascia board to give the correct fall to the gutter. The gutters clip into the supports, and, if properly assembled will not work loose by the action of wind, or by the impact of ladders or the weight of ladder and man. Care must be taken to avoid impact damage when erecting ladders to plastics eaved gutters. Joints for gutters and pipe are designed to allow for linear expansion or contraction of the gutter or pipe as when warmed by sunlight or affected by changes of ambient temperature. Most systems use fixed supports at the ends of gutter lengths, with sliding supports at 900-mm intervals; expansion or contraction takes place between the fixed supports.

The seal at a gutter joint comprises an expanded rubber sealing strip (which gives long life) and is made by clipping the gutter into the sockets of connectors; no bolts or mastic are required. The seal is water-tight along its length and yet allows longitudinal movement of the gutter to accommodate expansion or contraction. The joints of the pipe for small-sized systems are not sealed, and are an easy fit.

(v) *Recommendations for safe fixing*

Supports for the pipe should be carefully fastened to the wall, so as to ensure that no twisting or distortion is subsequently caused by misaligned fixing holes. They should have a maximum spacing of 2-m for vertical pipes, and non-corrodible screws and brackets should always be used in order to ensure that the life of the fixings is similar to that of the gutter and pipe. Most manufacturers supply suitable screws with their systems. Overtightening must be avoided so as to prevent any cracking of the plastics brackets and fixings.

Gutters and pipes are easily cut with a fine-toothed saw, and the fitting of short lengths is no problem. Conversion pieces from unplasticised PVC to cast-iron or cement-asbestos systems are available so that renovation and repair of existing systems with unplasticised PVC gutter or pipe is not difficult.

(vi) *Flow rate*

An unplasticised PVC $4\frac{1}{2}$-in nominal (11.45-mm) half-round gutter has a maximum flow rate of about 50 litre/min when fixed level within the discharge limits, and about 70 litre/min when fixed to a fall of 25-mm in 15-m. The smooth, non-corroding and growth-free surface enables these flow rates to be maintained during the life of the gutter.

(vii) *Maintenance*

Unplasticised PVC rainwater systems require no painting. If non-corrodible metal fastenings are used to secure the gutter and pipe to the building, maintenance is reduced to a periodic cleaning to remove dust, grit and other obstructions from the gutter.

(j) Underground Drainage

(i) *General*

The chemical industry has for many years used PVC, acrylonitrile-butadiene-styrene (ABS), polyethylene, and polypropylene pipes for various forms of effluent system, and relevant information is given in EEUA Handbook No. 20 "Thermoplastics Pipework and Ducting in Unplasticised Polyvinyl Chloride and Polythene" (Constables).

Continuous discharge of hot effluents, especially at temperatures approaching 100°C has a detrimental effect on PVC; ABS or polypropylene should therefore be used where large discharges of effluent at high temperatures may occur.

More recently work has been carried out to devise an underground drainage system to convey normal domestic effluents, including surface water — and B.S. 4660 (Unplasticised PVC Undergound Drain Pipe and Fittings) covers 100-mm (4-in) and 160-mm (6-in) sizes with fittings and accessories. The Standard anplies to drains laid under fields, yards, driveways, gardens and residential roads where depth of cover does not exceed 4-m. It does not cover the use of PVC drainage systems under main roads as these are more likely to be subject to heavy traffic loads.

Pipe for drainage is normally supplied in 1-m, 3-m and 6-m effective lengths, with sockets. Jointing is usually by rubber ring joints of either an "O" or "D" section; solvent cemented joints are employed where appropriate.

(ii) *Handling and storage*

As already explained in sub-section (b) (iv), on page 76, unplasticised PVC pipes are light and easy to handle and this can lead to abuse in some circumstances. The handling and storage methods outlines in that sub-section should therefore be adopted, and the same precautions observed.

(iii) *Installation and back-filling*

The installation and back-filling of unplasticised PVC underground drainage systems should always be carried out in accordance with the manufacturer's instructions. Owing to the flexibility of unplasticised PVC pipes, it is essential to provide them with adequate side support from the back-fill material. Trench widths should therefore be kept to a minimum, while 'as dug' material should be used for back-filling in the immediate vicinity of the pipe only if the compaction factor and particle size are suitable*. If not, then a material such as pea gravel or 5-mm to 10-mm broken stone should be used to form a 100-mm bed under the pipe, for side-fill, and to provide a cover over the pipe. 100-mm layers of 'as dug' material can then be successively laid and hand-rammed, Mechanical rammers should not be used until the pipe has at least 0.3-m of cover.

Bricks, wooden pegs or other levelling devices should not be left under the pipe or fittings, and all positioning struts or pegs at the side of the pipe should be removed before the trench is back-filled.

(iv) *Inspection chambers*

Half-section straight manhole channel and channel junctions, as well as half and three-quarter channel bends are available for the construction of inspection chambers. The external surfaces of the channels should be adequately roughened to provide a good key for mortar bedding and benching. Alternatively, preformed plastics inspection chambers may be used. These are designed to complement the unplasticised PVC drainage pipe.

* (See Ministry of Housing and Local Government's publication: "Working Party on the Design and Construction of Underground Pipe Sewers, Note of Guidance on Practical Considerations in the Structural Design, and in the Construction of Small Diameter Sewer and Drains".HMSO 1967).

Fig. 8/8(a) Combined soil and drainage inspection chamber (in ABS moulding).

Fig. 8/8(b) Inspection chamber – preformed from glass-reinforced plastics – with inlets
and outlets moulded into base (for use with PVC pipes).

Three different designs of chamber are available. The first, depicted in Fig. 8/8(a) is a moulding reproducing the channel and benching of the normal rectangular inspection chamber with an inlet and outlet on the main channel with two side inlets each side. It is connected to the drainage system, the space under the moulding then being packed with wet concrete, thus saving the cost of benching by hand. The walls of the chamber must be constructed in the usual way.

The second type (Fig. 8/8(b)) is in the form of a circular tub with inlets and outlets and channels moulded into the base; several invert layouts are

Fig. 8/8(c) Inspection chamber – unplasticised PVC merscar bowl with single-bottom outlet.

available. It should be bedded in 100-mm of granular material or concrete, and back-filled with selected material free from large stones. This chamber can support a vertical load of at least three tonnes; the cast-iron cover complies with B.S. 497 (Cast Manhole Covers, Road Gully Gratings and Frames, for Drainage purposes) for Grade 'C' covers and frames.

The third type is of a radical design, (Fig. 8/8(c)) comprising a simple unplasticised PVC bowl, with a single bottom outlet connected to the drain by an unplasticised PVC pipe that joins the main drain by means of a branch. The bowl is close to the surface; access to it from foul or storm-water drains is obtained simply by cutting a hole in the wall of the bowl, (using the special tools provided) at the most convenient point, and cementing-in the appropriate inlet connection. The drains and access pipe are back-filled, using well compacted granular material as detailed above; the bowl is bedded in concrete built up to ground level, using a variable-length collar extension on the bowl. The cast-iron cover and frame rest directly on the concrete.

(v) *Rodding*

When necessary to clear blockages in unplasticised PVC drains, care should be taken that any rods or equipment used are of a type that will not damage the pipes. Some of the conventional rodding implements, such as screw rods, could do this. A recent innovation is to use a 30-m coil of 12.5-mm (0.5-in) polyethylene tube for rodding and testing purposes. The coil, complete with reel and stand is available commercially and its use reduces the chances of damaging the unplasticised PVC pipe.

It is sometimes difficult to detect the presence of plastic pipes. These should therefore be brought right up to the rodding access so that they may be readily seen; the inspection chambers referred to in the preceding subsection (iv) may help in this respect. For simple systems, a surface rodding eye in unplasticised PVC is available; this is nothing more than a sealed access to the underground drain, designed to take rodding equipment.

(vi) *Road gullies*

Road gullies with or without traps, are available in moulded polypropylene. These are light (7 kg), unbreakable and can be stacked inside one another for storage. They are bedded and surrounded in concrete in the usual way, and do not require special lifting equipment to place them; in fact they must be held in place by being filled with water while being concreted in (see Fig. 8/9). They can also be used with unplasticised PVC underground drainage or with conventional drainage systems.

(vii) *Economic considerations*

Unplasticised PVC drainage systems cost more in *materials* than conventional systems. They are laid in longer pipe lengths however, jointing is easier, and the *total cost*, laid and back-filled, has been shown to be slightly less than for conventional systems. The greater the complexity, the greater the savings to be expected.

(k) Electrical Services

(i) *Cables*

The criteria for a good cable insulating material vary with the applications; but not all criteria apply with equal force when selecting a polymer for a particular type of cable. For example, it is only for power cables at 6.6 kV and higher voltages that care is necessary in selecting materials primarily for their electrical properties, especially for low dielectric loss angle and for high resistivity.

Fig. 8/9 Lightweight (polyolefine) drain gully.

For most low-voltage industrial cables, the emphasis is on mechanical properties, ease of manufacture and low cost. In building applications, plasticised PVC is the insulating material generally used, because of its low cost, availability, and ease of manufacture.

(ii) *Cable trays*

More use is now being made of PVC and polyethylene in the manufacture of of cable supports, cleats and trays; their resistance to chemical attack and their comparative cheapness make them a satisfactory alternative to metallic materials in most instances.

(iii) *Conduit*

Conduit systems made from plastics (and in particular PVC) are being used increasingly by the building industry in Britain as a direct replacement for steel. This practice has long been common in European countries, particularly Scandinavia, Netherlands and Italy. PVC conduit has several advantages in the building industry as it is adaptable equally to factory prefabrication or site installations. It is incorporated both in constructional slabs and dry partition walls. Its use is standard practice in industrialised building systems, particularly in those based on concrete.

Substantial savings can be made by using PVC conduit instead of steel, sometimes as high as one third of the total cost when both materials and installations costs are taken into account.

PVC conduit is covered by B.S. 4607 (Non-metallic Conduit and Fittings for Electrical Installations (Parts 1 and 2)). Part 1, Rigid PVC Conduits and Conduit Fittings, Metric Units, covers circular conduit only, and specifies two types, A and B. Type A is for use where installation is at temperatures not below $-5°C$, and Type B for use where installation temperatures are not below $-25°C$. The nominal sizes specified are 16-mm, 20-mm, 25-mm and 32-mm outside diameter, corresponding to the "Metric series" of sizes given in B.S. 3867 (Outside Diameters and Pressure Ratings of Pipe of Plastics Material) and in ISO Recommendation 161 (Pipes of Plastics Materials for the Transport of Fluids).

Part 2, Rigid PVC Conduits and Conduit Fittings, Imperial Units, of B.S. 4607 covers both circular and oval conduits. It specifies two types, Type AH, and Type AN, being high — and nominal — impact materials respectively, both of which are for temperatures not normally below $-5°C$. The nominal sizes for the circular conduit are $\frac{5}{8}$-in, $\frac{3}{4}$-in, 1-in and $1\frac{1}{4}$-in outside diameter; the oval conduits have major axes of the same dimensions with respective minor axes of 0.39-in, 0.45-in, 0.45-in and 0.45-in respectively. In addition, a 0.51-in by 0.32-in conduit is also available.

The circular conduit is produced in two wall thicknesses; heavy gauge and light gauge. The light gauge is suitable for suspended ceilings and where it is immediately buried in concrete. A wide range of fittings, connectors and boxes are available.

In neither Part of B.S. 4607 is an upper temperature limit specified but in general the conduit should not be used (unless completely encased in concrete or similar material) in environmental temperatures above 40°C, (see IEE Regulations for the Electrical Equipment of Buildings).

For cable conduit or ducts of larger sizes, PVC tube is available to B.S. 3506 (Unplasticised PVC Pipe for Industrial Purposes) in sizes up to 3-in nominal outside diameter. Special conduit (or duct) of a nominal $3\frac{1}{2}$-in diameter complying with a GPO specification can also be obtained. For installations where even larger diameters are required, ducts up to 12-in nominal, with $\frac{1}{8}$-in (3.3-mm) wall thickness can be supplied.

Flexible conduit, produced in 15-m coil lengths is made from corrugated rigid PVC. Such conduit is used where it can be concealed under plaster, or floor screeds or above ceilings. It is also employed for enclosing mains supply cables from eaves to meter positions, (where overhead electrical supplies are provided).

(iv) *Skirting, architrave and floor trunking*

A recent development, of particular interest to builders of offices and dwelling houses, is a variety of PVC trunking that can be fixed as skirtings

Fig. 8/10 Rigid PVC skirting duct (designed to accommodate electric cables), and socket outlet.

and architraves, and buried in the floor screed. Those designed as skirtings and architraves consist basically of two extruded sections, one a back section, fixed to the wall, and a front or face section which clips over the back one. Depending on the system, one of the sections is suitably shaped to accommodate cables (see Fig. 8/10). This type of trunking can also be fitted with an insert that allows low-voltage wiring (telephone wires, aerial leads) to be separated from power cables. The architraves usually run up to ceiling level to house the cables to be connected to the central lights. Socket outlets complying with B.S. 1363 (13-amp Plugs, Switched and Unswitched Socket-Outlets and Boxes), as well as light switches are integral with the skirting or architrave.

In office design, flexibility of partition is often required and open planning may be preferred. PVC trunking systems, available for assembly as underfloor ducts for electrical and communications services, offer the best planning flexibility, with the least structural change or damage to decorations. They also provide quick and easy access to the electrical services at all times during the life of the building, and comply with the IEE "Wiring Regulations" and GPO requirements for electrical and communications distribution in modern buildings.

(v) *Luminaires (Lighting fittings) and other fittings*

Luminaires, including those for fluorescent lamps with diffusers and those made to resist chemical attack, as well as sockets, plugs, switches and fuse boxes, are all available in plastics materials in a variety of shapes and sizes. Urea-filled formaldehyde or phenol-formaldehyde are generally used, the latter where dark-coloured fittings are specified. Plastics are not yet employed to any great extent for the large switches and fuse boards.

(vi) *High-voltage and medium-voltage switchgear*

There is growing use of epoxy resins as insulating materials in the construction of high-voltage and medium-voltage switchgear (up to 11 000 volts.)

(vii) *Earthing requirements*

Plastics are insulating materials and it is vitally important to take the following precautions when plastics pipes and fittings are installed: —

1. NO ATTEMPT SHOULD EVER BE MADE TO USE PLASTIC PIPE-WORK AS A MEANS OF EARTHING ELECTRICAL EQUIPMENT OR AS PROVIDING PART OF AN EARTH PATH.

2. WHERE PLASTICS PIPE REPLACES AN EXISTING METAL PIPE THAT HAS BEEN USED FOR EARTHING PURPOSES THE ELECTRICAL UNDERTAKING CONCERNED MUST BE ADVISED AT THE START OF THE WORK SO THAT ALTERNATIVE EARTHING ARRANGEMENTS CAN BE MADE TO ENSURE THE SAFETY OF PERSONNEL AND TO SAFEGUARD THE ELECTRICAL INSTALLATION AND ASSOCIATED PLANT.
   (See IEE "Wiring Rules" Section D, especially clause D 28(iii))

JOINTING AND SEALANTS

(a) General (and Glossary)

Joints in a building may be loosely classified in two types, i.e. construction joints, and movement joints as described in sub-section (b). The type of sealant used in each case depends on many factors some of the more important being described herein with reference to the recommended sealing materials.

Table 9/1 compares the properties of the more important sealants in current use, and a glossary of some jointing terms in the building industry is given in Table 9/2.

(b) Definitions of Joints

The two types of joint already referred to may be defined as follows:—

Construction joints: Those between different components resulting as a consequence of design, i.e. where a gap arises solely as a result of tolerances

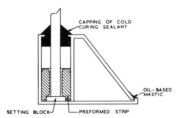

Fig. 9/1 Construction joints.

allowed in the components concerned, such as in day-joints in concrete and in a window frame, as indicated in Fig. 9/1.

Movement joints: Those which allow for expansion, contraction or differential settlement, such as the movement joints between sections of a curtain wall — see Fig. 9/2.

(c) Selection of Sealants

The type of sealant chosen for a particular joint depends in the first instance on how the joint is classified (see (a) above). Thus an expansion joint requires a rubbery seal, usually provided by a curing sealant of the silicone, polysulphide or polyurethane type. In contrast, a construction joint, with its correspondingly minimal movement can have a solvent based or non-curing material. Within these limits, choice can be further governed by other considerations such as

TABLE 9/1: COMPARATIVE PROPERTIES OF SEALANTS

(1) Sealant	(2) Type of change	(3) Pot-life	(4) Cure time (Drying time)	(5) Application methods	(6) Primers	(7) Operating temp. °C	(8) Toxicity (usual)	(9) Elongation maximum (Percentage)	(10) Tensile strength MN/m^2	(11) Hardness (Shore Scale A)	(12) Shrinkage (Typical percentage)	(13) Relative costs (Approx. with bitumen as unity)
Polysulphide (two-part)	Cure	Hours	Days	Pour Gun	Yes	−50 to 110	Oral	150 to 500	0.35 to 0.88	15 to 50	0.3	7 to 8
Polysulphide (one-part)	Cure	Not relevant	2 to 3 weeks	Gun	Yes	−50 to 110	Oral	100 to 250	0.35 to 0.88	15 to 60	<1	8 to 12
Epoxy (two-part)	Cure	Hours	Days	Pour Gun	No	−20 to 100	Dermal	5 to 15	14 to 70	90 to 100	Nil	4 to 6
Epoxy polysulphide	Cure	Hours	Days	Pour Gun	No	−20 to 110	Dermal	10 to 20	7 to 21	40 to 80	0.3	8 to 10
Polyurethane (two-part)	Cure	Hours	Days	Pour Gun	Yes	−55 to 90	Slight Dermal	250 to 450	0.35 to 1.4	10 to 40	Nil	4 to 5
Polyurethane (one-part)	Cure	Not relevant	2 to 3 weeks	Gun	Yes	−55 to 90	Slight Dermal	250 to 450	0.35 to 1.4	10 to 40	Nil	4 to 5
Silicone (two-part)	Cure	Hours	Days	Pour Gun	Yes	−60 to 120	Slight Dermal	50 to 250	2.8 to 4.2	20 to 50	0.1	12 to 14
Silicone (one part)	Cure	Not relevant	Days	Gun	Yes	−60 to 120	Slight Dermal	50 to 250	2.8 to 4.2	20 to 50	0.1	12 to 14
Acrylic (one part)	Thermoplastic	Not relevant	—	Hot Gun	Yes	−20 to 75	None	100 to 270	0.35 to 2.8	5 to 20	Nil	5 to 6
Butyl (one-part)	Solvent release	Not relevant	Days	Gun	No	−20 to 75	None	5 to 10	0.17 to 0.7	5 to 15	<5	2 to 3
Oil-based	Solvent release skinning	Not relevant	weeks	Gun	No	−10 to 70	None	5 to 50	0.035 to 0.14	5 to 10	<3	1 to 2
Bituminous	Thermoplastic	Not relevant	—	Pour Gun	No	−10 to 70	None	5 to 20	0.7 to 1.7	10 to 30	<1	1.0

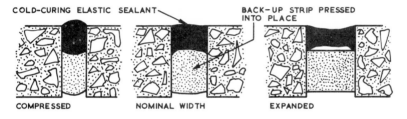

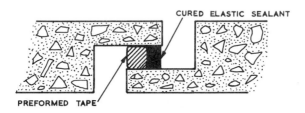

Fig. 9/2 Movement joints.

      Top: Expansion/contraction butt joint in concrete.

      Bottom: Lap shear joint in concrete.

ability to withstand traffic or chemical spillage (e.g. flooring joints), aesthetic value (e.g. colour, odour) etc.

The use and advantages of completely elastic or of completely plastic sealants requires careful consideration. In general those sealants with good elastic properties need stronger adhesion to joint surfaces in order that full use may be made of such properties, especially as the stretching forces may be quite high; the joint surfaces therefore need more careful preparation. In contrast, a permanently plastic sealant does not need such strong adhesive properties since the stretching forces, and corresponding extensions, are usually much smaller; these sealers therefore need a less complex preparation of joint surface. Their resistance to weathering and ageing however is often inferior to that of the elastic sealants.

(d) Application of Sealants

With all sealants the success of the sealing operation is very dependent on the quality of the sealant and the preparation of the joint surfaces as well as on the skill of application.

(i) *Surface preparation*

The preparation of the joint surface is particularly important. Owing however to the wide variety and combinations of surfaces to which a sealant may have to bond, no precise information can be given here on the surface preparation of the various materials between which a sealant joint may be required. In general, joint edges should be free of water, rust, dust, oils and soaps. Attention to this is very important with concrete jointing owing to the use of oils and mould release agents in cast work and the formation of a dusty

TABLE 9/2: GLOSSARY OF JOINTING TERMS

Term	Meaning
Sealant	A jointing material used as a filler, having particular properties in regard to low permeability (usually), high elasticity and adhesion (a description which may be applied to a wide range of jointing compounds)
Curing	A chemical process by which a sealant becomes hardened.
Elasticity	The property of recovering the original shape on release of a force causing deformation.
Mastic	A non-curing sealant.
Plasticity	The property of retaining a new shape after release of a force causing deformation.
Plastic deformation (a) Permanent set (b) Compression set	Terms which both indicate the permanent deformation of a sealant which has not regained its original shape completely after release of the deforming force.
(c) Creep (d) Cold flow	Terms which describe the mechanism within a sealant which results in permanent set.
(e) Stress relaxation	A stress-strain property of a sealant which causes creep resulting in permanent set.
Slump	Undesirable running, dripping, or sagging of a mastic or uncured sealant.

Application grades
    Gun grade
    Hand grade
    Pour grade
    Trowel grade
	
	Suitable for application by caulking gun
	Suitable for application by hand
	Suitable for application by pouring
	Suitable for application by trowel

Back-up strip	Inert material used to control the depth of application of a gun applied or poured sealant.

brittle "laitance" on the surface. (Having removed all these, the recommended primer must be applied where necessary as instructed by the manufacturer).

(ii) *Application skill*

The skill of application is also important; operations such as the thorough mixing of two-part materials, careful gunning to exclude trapped air, and correct application of backing material to control joint depth, are all vital in order to obtain a successful seal.

(iii) *Climatic considerations*

Even when all the previously mentioned requirements are met, adverse weather conditions can prevent an effective seal. Rainwater on a joint surface will impair adhesion, although some manufacturers provide primers that work effectively on damp surfaces. In any case, a surface should be free of water when the sealant is applied, Working in cold, (though dry) weather (i.e. below 4°C) is not recommended since condensation forms readily on joint surfaces.

(iv) *Handling and storage*

Care should also be exercised in the storage and handling of sealants, and their containers should be kept indoors away from heat. Some materials are listed as sensitive to water and must therefore be kept dry, but in all cases the manufacturer's storage instruction should be followed. Some sealants are inflammable or release toxic vapours or have slight dermatitic effects. As with the handling of any chemicals, cleanliness is also important.

(e) Flexible Sealants (see also Table 9/1)

The properties of some flexible sealants are summarised under sub-sections (i) to (ix) below, with reference to their performance, cost, precautions to be taken in some circumstances, and methods of application (including some disadvantages).

(i) *Silicones*

Performance: These high-performance sealants are for use in expansion joints and may be used in hostile environments. They have good low-temperature flexibility (down to −60°C), and are resistant to high temperatures (up to 150°C). They are also suitable for use in the presence of dilute acids and certain organic solvents.

Cost: Silicone sealers are still relatively costly.

Precautions: No toxicity rating when cured, though the uncured sealant may irritate skin and eyes.

Application: The sealants are usually supplied as one-component materials, although for certain applications two-component materials can be used: one-part silicone sealants are usually sufficiently fast curing to avoid the need for two-part materials. The sealants are gun-applied and primers may be necessary.

Disadvantages: High cost is the only disadvantage of a silicone sealant, though replacement should be correspondingly less frequent.

(ii) *Polysulphides*

Performance: These sealants have a relatively high performance, with excellent ageing resistance. They are good elastomers but somewhat plastic; to some extent this is an advantage since it relieves the stress at a joint which arises when there are slow variations of joint dimensions. No oxidation occurs with this polymer at normal temperatures; it also has good colour stability and shows little shrinkage.

Cost: Polysulphides are fairly expensive, although little more than half the price of silicones.

Precautions: Polysulphide sealants are often rated as having an oral toxicity hazard as they may contain lead or barium compounds.

Applications: Both one-component and two-component systems are available. One-component polysulphides can be used only where joint size and percentage movement are minimal, since slump can occur where the uncured material is subjected to large movements. Priming is usually recommended, especially for porous surfaces or where a bonded surface may be exposed to ultra-violet light.

Disadvantages: The most noticeable with polysulphide sealants are the need to mix two components together thoroughly, and, with a single-component material, the relatively long curing time – a matter of weeks.

(iii) *Polyurethanes*

Performance: This is comparable to that of a polysulphide sealant, though the cold creep (plasticity) is less.

Cost: Polyurethanes are much cheaper than polysulphide sealants.

Precautions: Cured polyurethane is non-toxic but the uncured material may irritate the skin.

Application: The sealant is usually supplied as a two-part system requiring mixing before application. Handling and storage are fairly critical since the presence of moisture may cause gelling during storage, or foaming of the mixed compound. Primers are generally required with these sealants.

Disadvantages: These lie in the detrimental effects of the presence of water.

(iv) *Acrylics*

Performance: Acrylic sealants have a lower performance than chemically curing types. They are thermoplastic and therefore subject to some cold flow which limits their application in large moving joints (because of the slumping which occurs).

Cost: These sealants are inexpensive, but this is offset by a corresponding reduced performance.

Precautions: Although acrylic sealants have low oral toxicity, prolonged skin contact should be avoided.

Application: These sealants must be applied hot. Primers are generally unnecessary.

Disadvantages: These are the need to heat before application (so as to make the sealant soft and plastic), and the tendency for the sealant to flow in large vertical joints.

(v) *Butyls*

Performance: The plastic nature of a dried butyl sealant makes it unsuitable for large moving joints, though it is ideal for design or system joints, e.g. as a bedding compound for glazing. Some shrinkage occurs on drying.

Cost: Butyl sealants are much cheaper than acrylics, and only slightly more expensive than the oil-based sealants referred to below.

Precautions: Butyl sealants are usually non toxic but contain a solvent which *can be* toxic and flammable: a heavy concentration of the solvent vapour may be a fire risk. The vapour should not be inhaled, and smoking in the area should be restricted.

Application: These sealants are easy to handle and apply, and primers are generally unnecessary.

Disadvantages: Can be used satisfactorily only where there is limited joint movement.

(vi) *Oil-based sealants*

Performance: Although Table 9/1 indicates that oil-based sealants have a lower performance than butyls, this is not necessarily always true since the two types operate differently. The oil-based form a tough leathery skin in a few days though the centre can remain sticky and plastic for years.

Cost: The oil-based are the cheapest gun-grade general purpose sealants now available.

Precautions: Oil-based compounds generally have low toxicity hazards, though some may contain lead.

Application: These sealants are applied direct to the joint surfaces, and primers are unnecessary.

Disadvantages: The cheaper of these oil-based sealants may suffer from a bleed out of oil into adjoining masonry, wood, etc. The soft interior can also give rise to an unsightly joint, if damaged.

(vii) *Bituminous sealants*

Performance: These sealants are usually suitable only in systems and design joints where movement is strictly limited. Their resistance to oils and some solvents is low.

Cost: They provide one of the cheapest sealing methods available.

Precautions: No serious hazard is involved; there may be a fire risk on heating, and the usual safety precautions should be taken when using gas burners.

Application: Bitumen sealants are generally supplied as single-component hot-applied (in a liquid state), and as such are widely used for sealing horizontal joints in floors and roofs.

Disadvantages: These sealants, being thermoplastic, become soft and possibly sticky in hot weather. Grit build up by adhesion to surfaces can weaken the material in the joint.

(viii) *Polyisobutylene (PIB) sealants (non-hardening)*

Performance: These sealants are generally in the form of extruded beads or strips. When used alone, they are suitable only for nonmoving constructions and system joints; owing to their plasticity they cannot be used in moving joints. They have good ageing resistance, with little shrinkage, and are unaffected by ultra-violet light, or water. An example of a riveted overlap joint is depicted in Fig. 9/3.

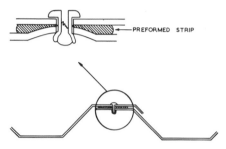

Fig. 9/3 Riveted overlap joint with PIB (non-hardening) sealant.

Cost: PIB-based sealants are very economical; not only is the product inexpensive on a cost-comparison basis, but the use of preformed strips greatly reduces wastage and handling costs. They can greatly reduce sealing costs when used in conjunction with other sealants.

Precautions: PIB sealants are non-toxic and may be safely handled.

Application: These sealants are often used for back-up material when sealing joints in conjunction with other sealants. They are commonly applied for example as a bedding compound for glazing, where a final capping compound of a high-performance sealant provides the weather proofing.

Disadvantages: Since this class of compound is permanently tacky, it readily picks up dust and dirt when exposed.

(ix) *Preformed foam strips (non-hardening)*

Performance: These foam strips are used solely as a secondary seal where waterproofing and airtightness are not essential. They prevent the ingress of dust and other contaminants through a joint, though their main application is in conjunction with other sealants (see previously mentioned Fig. 9/1). Types of foam that may be used include polyethylene, polypropylene, polyurethane, neoprene or epoxy-resin rubber, i.e. any inexpensive inert resilient foam. Inertness (e.g. to solvents in a capping compound and/or primer) as well as resilience is essential in order to hold the foam in place especially where joint movement occurs before final sealing.

Cost: Preformed foam strips are very cheap and are used to reduce costs on an expensive sealing compound by controlling the joint depth and reducing wastage.

Precautions: The only hazard presented by preformed foam strips is a slight fire risk, since they are all more or less combustible, depending on polymer type and foam structure.

Application: Application is extremely simple; the section is pressed into the joint, using a tool to control the depth of insertion. Various sections are available to cater for different widths of joint.

Disadvantages: The foam should be of a closed-cell structure to prevent the absorption of water which could otherwise interfere with joint movement when freezing occurs.

(f) Rigid Sealants

(i) *Epoxy resins*

Performance: These materials are often employed for grouting compounds when high chemical resistance and very strong adhesion are required. They are hard and inflexible, and cannot be used for joints where any movement may occur.

Cost: Epoxy resins are expensive and need only be used when full advantage can be taken of their good chemical resistance and strong adhesive properties.

Precautions: Uncured epoxy resins and curing agents should be carefully handled, as they can irritate the eyes, skin and nose; when cured they are non-toxic.

Application: These resins are supplied as two-component materials which need to be thoroughly mixed before being applied by gun, trowelling, pouring or grouting.

Disadvantages: High cost.

(ii) *Epoxy polysulphides*

Performance: These polysulphides combine the high strength and adhesion of the epoxy resins with the flexibility of the polysulphides. The flexibility is limited however (typically 5 per cent maximum) and these sealants should not be used for moving joints. They provide excellent seals for design or system joints where movement is small, especially where a good surface finish is required.

Cost: As with epoxies, these sealants are expensive and need only be used when full advantage can be taken of their properties.

Precautions: They should be carefully handled as some components of the resin and curing agent may irritate eyes skin and nose if contact is prolonged.

Application: Epoxy polysulphides are supplied as two-part materials, and after mixing are generally gun applied. Primers are not required.

Disadvantages: High cost is the main objection.

SECTION TEN

ADHESIVES

(a) Introduction

The old glues based on animal or vegetable substances have now been largely replaced by new adhesives based on plastics, synthetic resins and synthetic rubbers; such adhesives are described in this Section. They are available generally as solutions, as dispersions in water, or in the form of two or more components that have to be blended before application and bonding.

These new adhesives are being increasingly used in the building industry because:—

1. Certain types of mechanical fittings can be more readily secured than by screws, bolts, etc.

2. Strong joints can be made between a variety of materials.

3. The growing use of plastics in building creates a need for adhesive joints.

4. Industrialisation (prefabrication) of the building industry also leads to a wider application of adhesive joints.

When glueing various materials, it is important to use the type of adhesive recommended by the manufacturer for the purpose.

(b) Types of Adhesive

These may be conveniently described under the following subdivisions:—

(i) *Non-reactive systems*

These contain chemical substances which do not react chemically in the glueing process. The adhesives should be in liquid form so as to wet the surfaces to be glued together, and for this reason may be a colloidal dispersion or a solution. If the objects or materials to be treated are porous, they can absorb the solvent; if not, a contact adhesive should be used and the solvent allowed to evaporate before the pieces are brought together and pressure applied to obtain proper adherence.

Thermoplastic materials may also be used without solvent as melt adhesives. They are applied cold and heated, or hot applied, and will solidify again when the joint has cooled down.

(ii) *Reactive systems*

Another method is to use compounds which are applied as liquids of low molecular weight, and become high-molecular weight solids as a result of chemical hardening (curing). Such a process is generally unaccompanied by critical changes in volume or by the development of internal stresses. There are two processes in which compounds of low-molecular weight react chemically in the formation of an adhesive bond. In the first process two or more components are mixed before use, one being a curing agent or catalyst. They react slowly at room temperature, but at higher temperatures the reaction proceeds more quickly. In the second, there is only one component, and in this some cross-linking has already taken place. The adhesive bond is obtained at room or elevated temperature and pressure.

(iii) *Combined systems*

In order to obtain a strong adhesive bond, the adhesive layer should not be too brittle, compared with the parts to be bonded. For this reason thermo-setting compounds, when used as glues, are sometimes combined with thermo-plastics. For example, phenolics may be combined with polyvinyl chloride, or acetate. The presence of the latter prevents extreme cross-linking which would lead to the formation of a brittle material.

(c) Nature of the Bond Obtained

Adhesion between glued parts can be obtained in several ways, one being by mechanical adhesion. Here, the bond is made by glue penetrating into the porous surfaces of the mating parts. It is possible in some cases that the glue penetrates by partly dissolving (or swelling) the material to be bonded.

If however the objects to be glued are smooth and non-porous so that the glue cannot penetrate, the bond must be provided by inter-molecular forces. In such cases the materials to be bonded and the adhesive must be of similar chemical type, e.g. for polar materials, polar groups are required in the adhesive; while non-polar adhesives are necessary for the bonding of non-polar materials.

(d) Recommended Practices When Using Plastics Adhesives

The main factors to be considered when using plastics adhesives together with the precaution which should be taken are summarised in the following sub-divisions:—

(i) *Manufacturer's instructions*

New technology is constantly being developed and it should be borne in mind that many brands of each type of adhesive are on the market, often compounded differently to obtain specific properties. For this reason, the manufacturer's instructions should be carefully followed.

(ii) *Surfaces to be bonded*

It is important to ensure that the surfaces to be bonded are clean and free from dust. For most adhesives, the surfaces need to be dry though a few modern adhesives can be used on damp masonry or brickwork. Surfaces con-taminated by oil or grease should be degreased before bonding. Adhesion to smooth surfaces can be improved by prior roughening with emery paper, sand paper, or preferably with a coarse file.

(iii) *Applying the adhesive*

For work on building sites, simple methods of application are the best. Whilst a brush is the traditional tool for applying adhesives, and is still widely used, many adhesives are now applied by a trowel or a simple scraper. Some are supplied in cardboard cartridges for application by a hand-operated gun. For applications off a building site, blade spreaders, rollers coaters or spray techniques are often used. Equipment of this type is most useful where large areas are to be bonded and for repetition jobs.

It is essential to obtain a uniform application of the adhesive in as thin a layer as possible, and to ensure that there are no unfilled gaps between the surfaces.

(iv) *Handling two-part adhesives*

Correct proportioning of two-part adhesives is essential. Most adhesives of this nature are supplied in the correct proportions for mixing, but occasionally the two components are measured on site. Simple measuring devices are then required; accurate proportioning being more difficult under these conditions. The two parts can often be mixed by hand using a simple spatula; mechanical methods, if required, usually involve an electric drill fitted with a spiral mixing blade. For large-scale operations, equipment which meters and dispenses the adhesives in the correct proportions can be used.

It cannot be over emphasised however that *thorough mixing* and cleanliness of equipment are essential. It is particularly important to thoroughly clean out any unused, but partly-cured material from mixing vessels and containers, before new components are added; otherwise there is a risk that the partly-cured adhesive will cause the curing reaction to start prematurely in the freshly added components.

It is also important to ensure that mixed material is used within "pot life", and that no more material is mixed than can be used at one "go".

(v) *Applying pressure*

Instantaneous bonds are obtained with contact adhesive and sustained high pressures are not required. It is, however, essential to press the two mating surfaces firmly together so as to avoid the trapping of any air between them. Pressure is often applied by hand though a small hand roller may be used. With some adhesives, however, an instantaneous bond is not obtained, and the materials must, therefore, be clamped together until the adhesive has set — periods which may be short or last up to 24 hours. (Sufficient pressure should be applied to hold the surfaces in close contact throughout the setting time). For operations away from the building site, a mechanical press or a pair of nip rollers can be used to apply the necessary pressure.

(vi) *Curing or maturing processes*

"Contact-bond" adhesives exert some strength immediately after bonding, probably about 20 per cent of their ultimate strength which may take a week to build up. Similarly, two-pack adhesives may cure to solid form within hours, but take much longer to reach complete cure. The necessary time lapse should be allowed before the structure is put into service.

(vii) *Effects of external conditions*

The application properties and performance of adhesives can be affected by temperature and humidity. With solvent-based and aqueous adhesives, the drying-time lengthens as the temperature falls, and shortens as the temperature rises; the "tack-life" is similarly lengthened or reduced. High-humidity conditions may extend the drying time, but tend to shorten "tack-life". With aqueous adhesives, high-humidity greatly retards the drying, and may cause some difficulty, particularly where large areas of material are to be bonded together. In high humidities care should therefore be taken to ensure the absence of any condensed moisture on the bonding surfaces.

Research is now being carried out by adhesive manufacturers to minimise the effects of atmospheric conditions, and to make the adhesive operation less sensitive to them.

(viii) *Hazards*

Many adhesives are flammable, some release toxic vapours and some have slight dermatitic effects. "Good Housekeeping", cleanliness of personnel and equipment must be stressed.

(ix) *Storage*

Adhesives can be adversely affected by being stored at temperatures outside the ranges recommended by the manufacturers, since irreversible changes can then occur and cause a gel to form (i.e. at high or low temperatures). The manufacturer's storage recommendations should therefore be closely observed.

The storage of flammable adhesives and cleaning solvents may be covered by statutory regulations; in case of doubt, H.M. Factory Inspectorate should be consulted.

(e) Adhesives for Specific Applications

(i) *Floor coverings*

Floor coverings are now often glued, dispersions of polyvinyl acetate or styrene-butadiene rubber being supplied in addition to the conventional adhesives.

Vinyl asbestos tiles are generally bonded by bitumen-based adhesives if moisture is likely to be present, but by polyvinyl acetate when the adhesive is not subject to dampness. A contact-adhesive of polychloroprene is also sometimes used. Contact-adhesives based on polychloroprene are widely applied, particularly for floor coverings of plasticised PVC in the form of strips or tiles. Some types of plasticiser when using polychloroprene, migrate from the PVC to the adhesive layer. In such cases, (after consulting the manufacturer) an adhesive based on a solution of nitrile rubber can be selected.

Simulated terrazzo tiles made from epoxy or polyester resin may generally be bonded with adhesives based on the same type of resin as the tile.

It is important that only the recommended adhesives be used on concrete sub-floors since moisture can affect the integrity of some adhesives bonds. In areas of extreme moisture concentrations (bathrooms, etc.) it is always preferable to use one of the resin-based or rubber-based adhesives.

(ii) *Wall coverings*

Plasticised PVC foils are affixed to walls with dispersions of polyvinyl acetate, polyvinyl propionate, polyacrylic ester or rubber. Rubber-based types are sometimes preferred because they are quick-drying and attain strength quickly. With some PVC films, there is a risk of the plasticiser migrating to the adhesive layer and causing it to soften. This risk is precluded with adhesives based on nitrile rubber.

Rigid decorative laminates (melamine-phenolic) are being employed in tile and sheet form. They may be bonded with a neoprene-rubber-based contact-adhesive.

Plastics wall tiles from high-impact polystyrene or filled plasticised PVC are only a few millimetres thick and may be applied butt jointed, — no grouting between tiles is necessary. Adhesives may be based on polyvinyl acetate or rubber. When cleaning the adhesive from the tiles, solvents which may attack the tiles should not be used.

If rigid PVC sheets are to be bonded to a firm base, then an elastic adhesive (such as a compound based on rubber) should be used because of the high expansion coefficient of PVC. If the sheets have to be applied to a wooden framework, PVC adhesives, dispersions of polyvinyl acetate, or polyvinyl propionate, or contact-adhesives based on polychloroprene can be employed.

(iii) *Bonding of other materials*

Synthetic-resin additives increase the adhesive power of the cement mortar used for securing ceramic tiles and panels to brickwork concrete, and similar surfaces. To obtain better bonding properties, however, a mortar based entirely on resins should be employed. If the surface is smooth, adhesives can be used to affix tiles or panels but compounds based on natural or styrene-butadiene rubber can also be applied if the surface is not smooth. If ceramic panels are large and heavy, adhesive joints capable of exerting greater adhesive forces should be employed; mortars based entirely on polyester or epoxy resins should then be used.

Hardboard, plywood, and similar materials are often applied by adhesive to plaster surfaces. The usual adhesives for indoor use are dispersions of polyvinyl acetate or polyvinyl propionate. If a contact-adhesive is required then one based on natural rubber or polychloroprene should be chosen. For outside work, asbestos cement panels can be bonded to a wooden framework with resorcinol adhesive, heavy asbestos-cement panels (thicker than 6-mm) being secured by means of epoxy resin mortars.

Insulation materials are positioned by adhesive or clips, secured to the surface to be insulated by contact-adhesives of dispersions of polyvinyl acetate acetate, polyvinyl propionate or natural rubber.

Acoustic panels or tiles are sometimes bonded with contact-adhesives based on polychloroprene.

Polystyrene foam can be bonded with dispersion-type adhesives or with adhesives in which alcohol is used as a solvent. Many solvents attack the foam though polyurethane foam is resistant to some. It is sometimes bonded with polyurethane or epoxy-resin based adhesives. Adhesive joints for plastics pipes are dealt with in Section Eight.

(iv) *Bonding of structures*

There are many applications for adhesives in construction work, e.g. composite wooden girders and trusses, which are often bonded with resorcinol-formaldehyde adhesives. Concrete elements can be joined by epoxy or polyester mortars, but pretreatment is important and the concrete should be dry. The tensile strength of epoxy mortars is so great that the concrete will fail outside the joint in the event of overloading, – a result that cannot occur with polyester mortars.

Epoxy resin mortars are also used to bond steel and concrete. If old and new concrete are to be bonded, a cement mortar should be used to which plastic dispersions have been added to increase adhesion. Polyvinyl acetate, polyvinyl propionate, polyvinylidene chloride, acrylicesters, styrene butadiene or natural rubber dispersions are used for this purpose. A layer of epoxy adhesive is also applied to the old concrete and the new concrete is poured on when the adhesive begins to gel.

The bonding of metals is a specialised operation, only carried out in workshops. Polyurethane adhesives, epoxy adhesives, polymerizable acrylic ester or methacrylic ester adhesives can be used for these purposes.

SECTION ELEVEN

ADDITIVES

(a) Introduction

A hardwearing and durable finish can be obtained on concrete floors made from plain or air-entrained concrete, without resort to expensive admixtures to modify the properties of the concrete. Nevertheless, there are occasions when alternatives to the usual kinds of concrete for wearing surfaces must be considered. The chemical resistance, or resistance to oil absorption of an industrial concrete floor may be inadequate, but in some cases may be sufficiently improved by the use of a suitable admixture in a cement-bound floor topping. In others, where very aggressive chemicals are present, for example, more expensive non-cementitious compositions may be necessary.

The minimum thickness or ordinary concrete necessary for a floor topping on existing concrete is 100-mm (CP 204: In-Situ Floor Finishes). If worn concrete is to be resurfaced, it may first be necessary to remove a substantial volume of the old material before repair and re-surfacing can be effected (as the same level has normally to be maintained). A thin topping, with an adequate bond strength induced by a suitable admixture is attractive in such instances, but all problems associated with the preparation of suitable surfaces must be considered, particularly in relation to noise and dust arising from the use of mechanical scarifying equipment. It must also be remembered that in most cases, it is essential for old oil-soaked concrete to be removed before applying new material.

In this section information is given on the more common organic polymer/cement compositions now in use. Non-cementitious compositions are described in Section Seven. (Reference should also be made to EEUA Handbook No. 2: Flooring for Industrial Buildings.) IT MUST BE EMPHASISED HOWEVER THAT ORGANIC POLYMERS ARE FORMULATED FOR MANY APPLICATIONS AND THAT NOT ALL THESE PRODUCTS ARE SUITABLE FOR USE IN CEMENT COMPOSITIONS. THE MANUFACTURER'S ADVICE SHOULD BE SOUGHT BEFORE USING ANY PRODUCT WHICH IS NOT SPECIFICALLY MADE FOR THIS APPLICATION.

(b) Rubber Latex/Cement Compositions

(i) *General*

Natural rubber latex contains about 35 per cent rubber and 4 per cent protein as it comes from the tree. For commercial uses, it may be concentrated so as to have up to 75 per cent solids. The emulsions often contain added chemicals which act as stabilisers, preservatives, accelerators, antioxidants and vulcanising agents. Stabilised natural rubber latex is compatible with both Portland and high alumina cements, but more stabiliser is required with the former because of the coagulating effect of the free lime present in that type of cement. High alumina cement is preferred for mixing with a

117

rubber latex. Latex-cement compositions have been under development since 1930.

(ii) *Applications*

Emulsions, diluted with water, are suitable for use as gauging liquids for, (typically) 13-mm thick, 1:3 trowellable cement-mortar topping, levelling coats, as well as for patching worn areas of concrete. The minimum recommended thickness is 7-mm. A typical composition contains 15 per cent solids by weight of concrete. This material can be employed to lay jointless flooring in hospitals and schools and for light industrial uses not subjected to heavy traffic (such as steel-wheeled trucks), or to spillage of corrosive chemicals, oil, or grease.

(iii) *Properties*

Warm-feeling, resilient, dustless surfacing can be prepared from rubber-containing mortars. Natural rubber latex has the best rubbery properties of all the latexes with good tensile strength and dry-tack. After some months of ageing however there is some loss in resilience, and resistance to oil and grease is poor. Unrestrained flooring allows high moisture movement and drying shrinkage. Natural rubber latex can be loaded with more fillers than other latices, but as already indicated can be difficult to mix with Portland cement; heavy stabilisation is required and the products have a limited shelf life. Resilient, dustless non-slip toppings can be laid with natural rubber latices, but their poor resistance to oil, coupled with ageing changes (degradation) limit their use.

Reclaimed natural latexes and synthetic-rubber latexes are similar to natural rubber latex, but the cured compositions are generally weaker.

(c) Synthetic Resin Latex/Cement Compositions

(i) *General*

Polyvinyl acetate (PVAc) is the chief synthetic-resin latex at present employed in Portand cement compositions. PVAc dispersions are milky-white with about 55 per cent solids content in the most concentrated form. The resin may need softening with a plasticiser to improve the flexibility of the film; because of this, emulsions contain up to 20 per cent dibutyl phthalate. For the building industry, the manufacturers supply a general purpose emulsion with a 53–55 per cent solids content containing 10 per cent plasticiser.

Because of the inherent water sensitivity of PVAc, alternative materials in the vinyl class (PVAc copolymers and acrylic copolymers) have been introduced to replace it in flooring compositions.

(ii) *Applications*

1:3 mortar toppings, up to 13-mm thick, gauged with diluted resins can be laid on clean, dust free and oil free bases without resort to hacking to obtain a key. The mortars are of a viscous, trowellable consistency and can be laid in a jointless form and feathered. The optimum content of PVAc solids is 10 per cent weight of cement. Compositions for patching worn or spalled concrete can also be prepared from other synthetic resin emulsions.

(iii) *Properties*

PVAc increases the bond and tensile strength of mortar, while increased flexibility and resilience reduces the risk of cracking. The ultimate compressive strength of 1:3 cement: graded granite screed made with PVAc is about 17 MN/m^2. PVAc compositions offer good resistance to oil, petrol and grease. The dried composition is less rubbery than that made from natural rubber latex; it is water sensitive because of the water-soluble additions necessary for polymerisation. In damp environments, the film slowly re-emulsifies with a consequent loss in properties, e.g. the wet abrasion resistance becomes low.

Acrylic resin emulsions have similar properties to PVAc emulsions, and can also be mixed with cement though the dried films are not water sensitive. With machine mixing, over 20 per cent air may be incorporated in the mix. The addition of 0.5 per cent silicone oil reduces this unwanted air entrainment significantly, but this must be added as a separate component. The ultimate compressive strength of 1:3 cement: graded granite screed made with an acrylic emulsion is about 24 MN/m^2. Moderate resistance to aggressive chemicals is obtained with these resins, and their resistance to wear makes the toppings suitable for light industrial floors.

PVAc emulsions are relatively inexpensive and are readily available throughout the building trade. Compositions containing PVAc behave well on dry internal surfaces and on external vertical surfaces. They also have good bonding qualities with resistance to chemical attack by oil, though the oil will stain.

The water sensitivity of PVAc is a disadvantage, and for this reason the material is no longer being used in some fields, e.g. PVAc cannot be used in toppings externally on roadways. Acrylic films are better than PVAc films in permanently wet situations but the emulsions cost more and are not so readily available.

PVAc is however a useful emulsion, widely employed in the building industry for a number of purposes, such as a bonder in key coats, mixing with plaster, and as an adhesive, as well as for mixing with cement for flooring compositions. It is likely however to be superseded by all-acrylic emulsions in certain fields where moisture is troublesome.

(d) Polyester Resin/Cement Compositions

(i) *General*

Polyester resins are normally blended with styrene monomer, the solution being an unstable viscous liquid that slowly sets by itself after some months or years. Setting is accelerated by heat, light and by chemical additions.

Polyester resins cured by chemical additions have many uses with glass-fibre in the manufacture of glass-reinforced plastics laminates where production is closely controlled (See EEUA Handbook No. 21: Chemical Resistant Materials, Part 1). With inert fillers such as granite powder, china clay, etc. they have only limited applications in surfacings for floors, since the need for on-site mixing with critical proportions, combined with the material's relatively high cost and high shrinkage (as compared with Portland cement) limit their usefulness.

More recently, a Portland cement/polyester resin/styrene composition has been developed which overcomes most of the disadvantages of polyester resin alone. The composition is a viscous liquid that needs only the addition of water to initiate the setting reaction. The added water hydrates the cement, and the byproducts of this reaction catalyse the polyester and styrene; these then set to form a tough rigid polymer. The characteristics of this Portland cement/polyester resin composition are described below.

(ii) *Applications*

These polyester resin/cement compositions are binders for strong inert aggregates and can be employed for a full range of concretes and mortars. Economic factors however restrict their present use to dense mortar mixes with selected aggregates such as industrial floor toppings, concrete paving repairs, and jointing and surfacing building units.

Formulations are available for floor toppings which can be laid from 25-mm thick down to a feather edge (nominal 8-mm). Other mixes have been developed for general purpose applications as adhesives toppings for low traffic-density areas, repair of spalled joints and general surfaces of concrete.

(iii) *Properties*

Hardened products after 24 hr-setting have compressive strengths about the same as unmodified Portland cement mixes after 28 days. The tensile strengths are substantially higher than those of normal concrete, while adhesion bond strength to good concrete, timber or steel, is about 1 MN/m^2 in direct pull-off tests.

Shrinkage is approximately the same as that of unmodified Portland cement at the normal binder/aggregate ratios. The hardened product is water-proof (unaffected by water); it also resists most normal acids and alkalis, hydrocarbon fuels, oils as well as most materials commonly met. Reagents known to cause a reduction in strength are: chlorinated hydrocarbons, low-boiling cyclic hydrocarbons and ketones. Climatic conditions do not affect the useful properties; working temperatures between $-20°C$ and $+80°C$ are acceptable. Polyester-resin-modified Portland cement-concrete will burn but will not support combustion. Neither does it effloresce.

Polyester resin/cement compositions need only the addition of water to set them; they set rapidly with low shrinkage. Apart from the properties just mentioned, the hardened product also has high compressive and flexural strengths with good adhesive bond. Feather edges can be made with these compositions. The storage life is limited however, and the water addition (for setting) is critical. Equipment using them cannot be cleaned with water and a solvent such as acetone with its attendant fire risk must be applied instead.

Aggregates which use these compositions must be dry, and any surface to which they are to bond must be thoroughly degreased and scoured clean.

The present price of polyester resin/cement compositions is approximately thirty times that of Portland cement alone, but for certain specified applications (such as thin toppings to concrete floors, repair and surface treatment to concrete, and high-bond strength quick-setting mortars), they have considerable advantages over normal Portland cement to offset this higher cost.

(e) Economic Considerations

Polyester resin/cement compositions, as already indicated, are rather more expensive than the mortars they replace, but in view of their particular qualities, can be considered economically viable.

SECTION TWELVE

BUILDING ACCESSORIES

(a) Introduction

This section deals with building elements not covered by others. New uses
for plastics materials appear almost daily. Many are withdrawn after a short
time because they fail to establish a market, possibly because they do not
justify the claims made for them, are too expensive, or because the new techniques involved are not readily accepted by existing trades. In some cases,
experience is necessary, and there is reluctance to be too early in the field. On
the other hand, many new plastics applications are successfully established.

It is difficult in such a fluid market, to present a complete and reliable study
of building accessories, but the information in the following sub-sections covers
some of the ground and indicates the wide range of applications. Whenever a
new application is offered it should be checked against the schedule of characteristics given in this handbook (See Table 1/1 and Appendix A).

(b) Complete Units

Whole bathroom units have been made in acrylics and glass-reinforced polyester (GRP). A two-storey telephone exchange has also been made in GRP, and
phenolic resin foam. Heart units for blocks of flats and houses using many plastics

Fig. 12/1 Glass-reinforced polyester shelter.

122

Fig. 12/2 Contact moulded glass-reinforced polyester feeder pillar cubicle.

elements are also being fitted. Buildings have been erected with GRP facing panels incorporating windows and complete units made from GRP are coming into general use, e.g. small kiosks and shelters, swimming pools and changing cubicles. Large structures can now be erected completely in glass-reinforced polyester, typical examples being illustrated in Figs. 12/1 to 12/3. In all such cases however, steps must be taken to ensure that the structure can safely withstand prolonged exposure to weather as well as general usage.

Fig. 12/3 "Rondo" house, 8-m diameter, moulded in glass-reinforced polyester by
sandwich construction method.

(c) Plastics Panels and Facings

Unplasticised PVC weather boarding is made in a range of colours and
requires no maintenance, though assurance should be sought regarding colour
fastness as well as weather resistance and the fixing arrangements to allow for
thermal movement.

Thermoplastics materials (mainly melamine formaldehide, PVC fabrics or
film and various laminates), are used as facings to other materials, as well as for
wall coverings. Some are self-adhesive, but in other cases, it is important to use
the correct adhesive. Panels so faced are used for wall panelling, kitchen,
laboratory and lavatory fitments, lift lining, water closet partition, and for
similar purposes. They have the advantage of easily cleaned surfaces with a
durable colour and pattern. The adhesive used for plastics films or fabrics
laid on plaster contains a fungus inhibitor.

Cover strips in PVC are made in a wide range of types to cover butt joints, angles and edges.

Tiling and mosaic can be made in preformed panels in which the tiling is bonded to plywood backed by foamed polystyrene. Small units of tile or mosaic are omitted and fixed later, in order to allow the panel to be fixed by screws to the brick structure. Compressible polystyrene adjusts to an uneven surface.

(d) Transparent and Translucent Materials

These can be used as substitutes for glass. They can easily be cut away by burning and do not normally provide the same security as glass for external

Fig. 12/4 Plastics roof lighting (in moulded form).

windows. Acrylics, glass-reinforced plastics and PVC are employed where light transmission is required, their main advantages being lightness, easy to mould and form, and non-brittleness. Their high thermal coefficients of expansion render them unsuitable for use as large sheets, and their soft surfaces are easily scratched. When employed as substitutes for glass, the edges should be fixed so as to allow for thermal movements. Figs. 12/3 to 12/5 illustrate some of their applications in moulded form. When used for roof-lighting, they can be double-skinned for thermal insulation, clear or obscure. In some cases they are accepted by fire-brigade authorities as smoke vents, since acrylics and PVC are thermo-plastic and melt before the ignition temperature is reached.

Fig. 12/5 Plastics roof light with extraction fan unit (in moulded form).

(e) Sculptured Finishes

Expanded polystyrene in thick blocks can be carved to produce sculptured surfaces in concrete (when used as shuttering). Where a pattern is to be repeated,

Fig. 12/6 Sculptured concrete surfaces made from glass-reinforced plastics mould (polystyrene).

a glass-reinforced plastic mould can be made from the polystyrene and used many times (See Fig. 12/6). The glass-reinforced plastic mould itself can be used as a decorative panel when the work is complete. Finer work, suitable for internal surfaces can be carved in resin bonded chipboard (see Fig. 12/7).

Fig. 12/7 Finely carved resin-bonded chipboard as an internal surface.

Sculptured surfaces control weathering and enhance the otherwise drab appearance of weathered concrete. It is also claimed that they are economical for internal use since surface finishes need not then be applied to the concrete structure.

Sculptured finishes are gradually establishing themselves, and if they become widely accepted will influence architectural design. If this occurs the sculptor must become involved in the design at an early stage.

Polystyrene blocks can also be used on floor or roof shuttering to form shaped coffers (or recessed panels) which reduce the weight of concrete required, and form attractive ceilings. The top surface of the blocks can also be carved or hollowed to provide richer effects (see Fig. 12/8).

(f) Sanitary Goods

Acrylic, glass-reinforced plastics, polyethylene, and polypropylene has been used experimentally for urinal stalls. Plastics for this purpose have advantages in that they can form joint-free stalls, resistant to attack by urine and decomposition products and by cleaning and disinfectant chemicals. Such stalls have been tested for several years and are gradually being accepted, especially for schools and hospitals and where joint-free constructions are required in order to avoid the casual leakages that can occur by the corrosion of the cement grouting in other systems.

The use of baths made from vacuum-formed acrylic sheet is now well established, and costs compare favourably with those of stove enamelled, cast iron and pressed steel. They are available in white and also in a range of

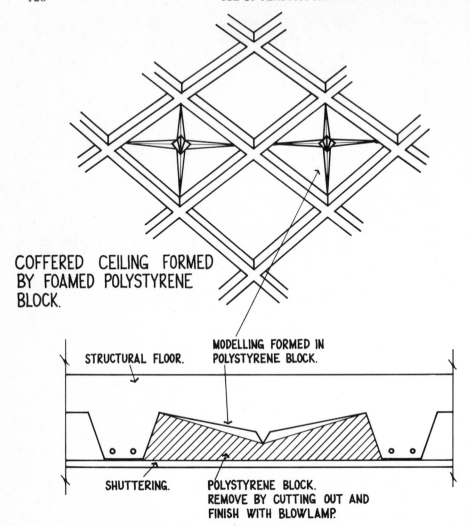

COFFERED CEILING FORMED
BY FOAMED POLYSTYRENE
BLOCK.

MODELLING FORMED IN
POLYSTYRENE BLOCK.

STRUCTURAL FLOOR.

SHUTTERING.

POLYSTYRENE BLOCK.
REMOVE BY CUTTING OUT AND
FINISH WITH BLOWLAMP.

Fig. 12/8 Coffered concrete ceiling formed by use of foamed polystyrene blocks.

colours (see Fig. 12/9). B.S. 4305 (Baths for Domestic Purposes Made from Cast Acrylic Sheet), covers the design, construction and dimensions of acrylic baths and specifies their rigidity with and without cradle. Their cleaning is best carried out with liquid detergents; abrasive powders are unnecessary and may scratch their glass-like surfaces. Cleaning instructions are normally given on labels stuck to the inside surface.

Shower trays and the walls of shower cubicals are made from both glass-reinforced plastics and vacuum formed acrylics. These materials provide light, easily installed cubicles with the minimum number of joints; the acrylics are warm to the touch and also available in a range of colours. (See Fig. 12/10).

Lavatory basins are made in acrylic and glass-reinforced plastics, but are seldom free standing, being generally combined with tabling to form "vanitory

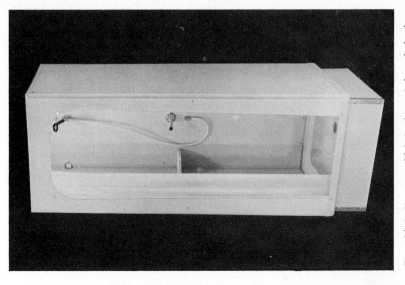

Fig. 12/10 Shower cubicle in glass-reinforced plastics.

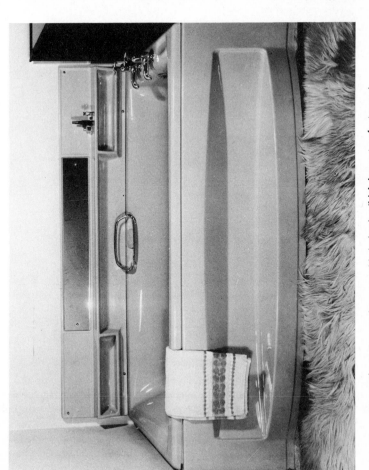

Fig. 12/9 Bath unit from moulded plastics (high-impact polystyrene).

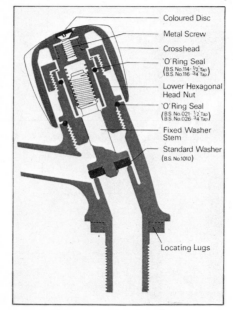

Fig. 12/11 Taps made from acetal copolymer.

Top:　　　For "hot" and "cold" supplies.

Bottom:　　Sectional view through tap.

units". Bathroom cabinets, soap dispensers, soap dishes, towel rails and other fittings are produced in a variety of plastics materials. All such items, as well as baths and shower cubicles, can however be marked by abrasive cleaners and by burning cigarettes.

Taps made from acetal copolymer (see Fig. 12/11) are available in white and in colours to match the sanitary colours of acrylic baths. These taps have non-rising spindles, and the washers seal with a non-rotational action thus extending their life. They are corrosion free, do not get hot when employed for hot water services, can be easily cleaned, and can be polished (with metal polish) if they become scratched. Similar designs are available for kitchens, including mixer taps, and stop-cocks are being developed. Knobs in distinctive shapes and colours can be supplied to identify taps or valves, (whether made from plastics or metal) as for example in laboratories or shower baths.

Cold water storage tanks are available in polyethylene and polypropylene to B.S. 4213 (Polyolefin and Olefin Copolymer Moulded Cold-Water Storage-Cisterns). They are either round or rectangular, completely corrosion resistant, and because of the material's low thermal conductivity do not "freeze" so readily. When fitting ball cocks and outlets, traditional thread-sealing compounds must not be used since these can cause cracking of the tank walls. The recommended thread seal in these instances is unsintered PTFE tape. Tanks of similar design are also available in glass-reinforced plastics, but care should be taken in selecting them to ensure that they have a good gel coat on the inside surface where water comes in contact with the resin.

Water closet cisterns have been made from a number of plastics; the most usual is a high-impact grade of polystyrene for the body and lid, and polypropylene for the syphon assembly. The ball cock is available in acetal-copolymer, and the ball float in polyethylene or polypropylene; the only metal remaining in these appliances being that for the flushing mechanism and ball-float arm. This nearly all-plastics system provides excellent corrosion resistance and a maintenance-free service.

Water closet seats to B.S. 1254 (Water Closet Seats, Plastics), are generally made from phenolic or amino-thermosetting materials, and are available in matching colours as well as in black or white. Other materials such as polyethylene and polypropylene have also been used but not to any extent so far, despite their advantages of lightness and ease of cleaning.

(g) Door and Window Fittings

Door handles, knobs and push plates in a range of colours are made in phenol formaldehyde, polyvinylchloride (plasticised), PVC-coated brass or steel or nylon-coated steel. They are generally cheaper than those of brass, aluminium, or bronze, but choice is often determined by appearance and life expectancy. The cheaper qualities will not be as serviceable as the dearer. Nylon ball-catches and hinges are smooth and silent and need no lubrication. Plastic hinges are not permitted on fire doors however, but straps of nylon, polyvinylchloride (plasticised), or polypropylene are suitable as hinges for traps and hatches, since they can be flexed an infinite number of times and operate smoothly after long idle periods.

Sliding door gear in nylon is common for light-duty and medium-duty doors, because it is silent and smooth running; it is used extensively for cupboards, showcases and glass doors. Plastic fabric facing for collapsible doors is now much employed, for it has a pleasant appearance and does not spoil with continuous folding. Curtain rails and runners in polyvinylchloride (plasticised) or nylon are available in many variations, sometimes in combination with aluminium; some types have been known to become brittle when located above radiators.

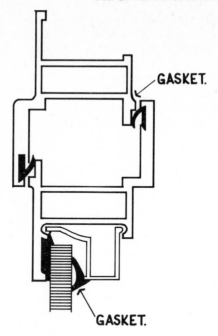

Fig. 12/12 Neoprene gaskets as draught checks and sealing in metal-framed window (see also Figs. 4/30 and 4/31).

Draught excluders, generally in neoprene, are used with wood and metal doors and windows. Fig. 12/12 (as well as Figs. 4/30 and 4/31) depict variations of neoprene gaskets used as draught checks and glass seatings for metal framed windows. Most metal window manufacturers now use this feature in some form.

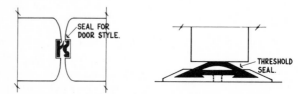

Fig. 12/13 Neoprene draught checks for wooden doors.

Fig. 12/13 depicts two uses of neoprene as draught checks with wooden doors; there is a wide range of checks for different situations.

Nylon bushes are used extensively for bearings in moving parts of windows.

(h) Stairways

Handrails can be made in polyvinyl chloride (plasticised), fixed on site by clipping it over a metal core rail, or alternatively, fixed to the rail by a shrinking technique; in this case, heat applied after placing the capping in position, enables the capping to be shrunk on to the core. It can be swept around bends and wreaths and rarely becomes detached.

Stair nosings are also made in plastics materials or as plastics fillings (polyvinyl chloride (plasticised) or neoprene) for aluminium. The filling is generally in the form of a flat or ridged insert to take the wear of footfalls. Such nosings besides preventing wear of the step edge are also attractive in appearance.

(j) Signs and Letterings

Plastics lettering moulded and cut from phenol formaldehyde or PVC-coated metal, with secret fixing, is used for fascias and name plates. Illuminated fascias

Fig. 12/14 Illuminated fascia of translucent acrylics
Top: Direction notice   Bottom: Advertisement

are often made of translucent acrylics (see Fig. 12/14). Some colours tend to fade and the makers advice should be sought. Signs incorporating the lettering in the panel are also made in glass-reinforced plastics.

(k) Plastics-Coated Metal

PVC-coated metal has many uses, especially when something better than paint is required. Coloured dresser hooks or cloak room hooks are a characteristic use. In atmospheres where significant condensation can occur, plastics-coated hook bolts prevent corrosion of the bolt and the formation of rusty drippings where asbestos sheeting is used. (In general plastics-coated hook bolts with caps at the ends of the bolts protect against rust, and reduce rust stains). Plastics-coated metal is also available for glazing bars, but it should be remembered that, if the plastics coating is damaged, the metal underneath may corrode unnoticed.

Grilles are available in nylon and nylon-coated metal. A common form is a perforated nylon curtain which allows scope for a wide variety of design.

(l) Other Uses of Plastics in Building Accessories

Other uses of particular plastics materials are briefly described below:—

(i) *Neoprene and nylon*

Neoprene is employed to form resilient bearings as indicated in Fig. 12/15. Tap washers of neoprene and nylon are commonly used, but those of nylon

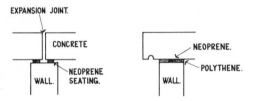

Fig. 12/15 Neoprene resilient slab bearing.

sometimes become compressed and lose their effectiveness. Nylon fixing plugs for screws are also widely used.

Expanded polystyrene when employed as an external filler should be protected to prevent its removal by birds for nesting purposes.

(ii) *Glass-reinforced plastics*

These materials can be made up to suit individual requirements — Fig. 12/16 for example depicts a glass-reinforced plastics fascia used with a flat asphalt roofing.

(iii) *Plastics spraying*

Polyurethane can be sprayed in-situ to any required thickness to provide thermal insulation in difficult situations, e.g. under valley gutters. There is a delay of a few seconds before foaming is complete and it is not possible therefore to control the finished surface, which remains slightly rough-textured. Some "fall-out" occurs and toxic fumes are given off, so that the work should be programmed to be carried out when these two conditions are not critical. Good ventilation is essential when the material is sprayed in confined spaces.

A film of polyvinyl chloride (plasticised) and polyvinyl acetate (PVAc) can also be applied as a spray to form an impervious skin on other materials. It is

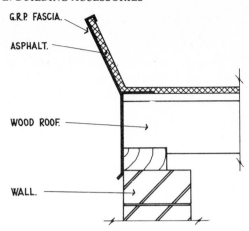

G.R.P. FASCIA.

ASPHALT.

WOOD ROOF.

WALL.

Fig. 12/16 Glass-reinforced fascia strip, used with flat asphalt roofing.

Fig. 12/17 Sprayed plastics skin on a brick wall.

Fig. 12/18 High-impact unplasticised PVC shutters.

Fig. 12/19 Section of wire-reinforced PVC louvres.

effective when used as a strip to cover joints in asbestos or similar material,
to stop draughts or the entry of dust or moist air. Some "fall-out" (with
some toxic fumes), also occurs during spraying, but although not generally
serious, should not be overlooked. Fig. 12/17 depicts such a skin on a brick
wall.

(iv) *Shutters, louvres, and blinds*

Roller shutters are available in high-impact unplasticised polyvinyl chloride
(PVC) in several colours, which can be assembled in colour combinations.
Fig. 12/18 illustrates this type of shutter. Louvres are made in wire-reinforced
PVC to provide a weatherproof section with good light transmission, one such
example being depicted in Fig. 12/19. Venetian blinds with nylon ribbons,
cords and pulleys, and with plastics-coated metal laths are popular for
domestic use. In all situations, the methods of keeping them clean should be
considered.

SECTION THIRTEEN

TEMPORARY AIDS TO BUILDING

(a) Introduction

This Section deals primarily with the use of plastics during building construction, little reference being made to the plastics components used in the building.

Plastics can improve the environment for those employed on a building site, and also provide better protection for existing structures and partially-completed sections of a project. By using them for the manufacture of contractors plant, better performance, reduced maintenance and greater durability can be obtained. Building components are often damaged during transport and storage on site. Plastics are therefore being more widely used as packaging and for covers to minimise damage resulting from rough handling and from deterioration under poor storage conditions.

(b) Weather Protection and Screening

It is often necessary to protect working areas from the weather and to isolate areas inside a structure by means of temporary screens. Construction costs and programme time can be much reduced if work can proceed during bad weather. The introduction of cheap, transparent lightweight plastics sheets has increased the use of plastics screens for such protective purposes.

(i) *Materials*

Polyvinyl chloride (plasticised) and glass-reinforced plastics in the form of rigid corrugated or flat sheets have advantages in some cases but their comparatively high cost restricts their use. More favoured as sheeting for temporary screens, are flexible films of plasticised polyvinyl chloride, polyethylene or other plastics obtainable in various thicknesses as rolls of plain film, or as eyeletted sheets with seamed edges for fixing by cordage to scaffold tubes, timber frames, or similar structures. If better tear-resisting qualities are required, films reinforced with wire or synthetic mesh can be employed. Transparent grades are available if light transmission is needed. The pigmented grades are generally more durable however and are better if light transmission is not required. The gauge of sheet and reinforcement selected for a particular application depends, amongst other items on the location, type of work, duration and economic factors. A typical example of the use of reinforced sheeting is indicated in Fig. 13/1. This depicts wire-reinforced cellulose acetate sheets, fixed to the outside of a scaffold, being employed to protect construction workers against the weather. A similar arrangement can be adopted to protect the public when construction work or cleaning may be a nuisance.

Fig. 13/1 Weather protection sheeting (wire-reinforced cellulose acetate).

(ii) *Shelter units*

Small shelter units are available to improve amenities for construction workers or to provide protection from the weather on small jobs; they generally take the form of sections or of complete units, made from glass-reinforced plastics, with or without frames.

(iii) *Precautions to be observed*

Some of the plastics used in these applications are flammable, and it is imperative to reduce fire risks to a minimum by the careful use of blow lamps, gas heaters and welding equipment etc., and by preventing the accumulation of combustible rubbish. As previously mentioned, plastics of a self-extinguishing grade with low flame-spread properties are available for use where a fire risk is high.

(c) Pneumatic Buildings

Plastics such as plasticised polyvinyl chloride, or coated-woven polypropylene are used for prefabricated bubble buildings inflated by continuously running low-pressure compressors. Buildings of this type have been made with floor areas up to 230-m^2, a typical example being illustrated in Fig. 13/2. Natural lighting inside can be provided by incorporating panels of translucent PVC in the walls. Access is obtained through air locks, but if vehicle traffic is high, an air curtain can be provided at the entry/exit in order to minimise pressure loss.

(i) *Advantages*

Some of the advantages of these inflatable structures are the absence of internal supports, and clean conditions inside (especially if the incoming air

Fig. 13/2 Pneumatic prefabricated "building" showing air-lock entry.

is filtered), the plenum effect excluding external dust and dirt. Air for inflation can also be heated to provide warmth in winter; for example the compressor unit to the structure illustrated in Fig. 13/2 includes a heater as well as a fan. Structures of this type can also be erected or dismantled quickly and are easily folded and stowed into a fairly light small packs for transport — properties that are extremely useful when frequent moves are likely.

(ii) *Operating requirements*

A reasonable seal must be provided at the periphery of these inflatable structures in order to prevent excessive loss of air. This can be done in several ways, depending on site conditions. The pressure needed to keep a structure properly inflated in position is quite small; 100 N/m² (0.0145 lb/in²) is sufficient for normal weather conditions, increased to about 150 N/m² to provide maximum wind resistance. The internal air pressures are not sufficient to withstand heavy snow loads (greater than about 100-mm deep), and heating should be provided to prevent snow accumulating on any inflatable building needed during the winter. Thermal conductance of the materials used is high, and condensation can therefore be a problem.

(d) Buildings with Pneumatic Frames

This type of pneumatic building is similar to those described in (c) above except that inflated tubes are used to support a fabric stretched between them; continuously-running compressors and air locks are therefore unnecessary. A tube puncture can cause collapse, but because of the form of construction, there is less chance of failure with this type of structure than one requiring internal air pressure to retain its shape.

There is no plenum effect, and if clean conditions are required inside, precautions similar to those with any traditional type of building must be taken to prevent the entry of dust and dirt.

(e) Plastics Used to Protect Construction Materials

Plastics are supplied in many forms for preventing damage to materials and components during transport and whilst being stored on site. As already indicated they can also be used to protect parts of a completed structure during construction.

Sheets and purpose-made mouldings of cellular plastics are often employed to protect fragile materials against mechanical damage. Polyethylene or plasticised PVC sheets are employed to protect against damp or dirt. Many articles are supplied in polyethylene bags, sealed to prevent deterioration from moisture; this method is particularly useful for packaging a number of small components. Cheap plastics sheets, made from polyethylene are readily available for covering bulk materials like timber, bricks, cement, aggregate and similar materials. Their low cost and lightness also promotes their use to protect materials which although not adversely affected by weather, are difficult to handle and use correctly when wet. Such sheets are also useful for covering equipment or materials during frosty weather; they do not have very good thermal insulating properties, but the air trapped under them helps to retain heat.

Foamed plastics slabs can be employed to protect against mechanical damage, and adhesive plastics tapes have been used for protecting special finishes. Care must be taken with some such tapes as they have been known to stain the finish.

The use of plastics sacks is becoming increasingly popular for delivering aggregates and similar bulk granular materials, as well as for the storage and removal of rubbish, especially where sites are congested or access is difficult.

(f) Temporary Pipework

Polyethylene, plasticised polyvinyl chloride (PVC) and nylon are used for above-ground and below-ground pipe systems for water drainage, compressed air and other liquids and gases. PVC is most suitable for rigid pipes; polyethylene or nylon for flexible pipes. The pipes are light, easily laid and can be taken up when no longer required. Water in a plastics pipe does not freeze so readily as in metal pipes; and if freezing occurs the damage to the pipe is usually less.

PVC and high-density polyethylene pipes are being increasingly used for pumping concrete around a site. As with steel pipes used for similar duties, quick-release joints to facilitate blockage clearance, rapid erection and dismantling are available. The impact strength of PVC is lower that that of polyethylene, particularly at $0°C$, though PVC is somewhat cheaper.

(g) Plastics and Formwork for Concrete

When using plastics in conjunction with formwork, there is a greater tendency for holes (resulting from air bubbles) to form on the surface of concrete cast against plastics coatings, than when cast against timber, steel or similar formwork.

(i) *Linings of polyethylene sheet*

Polyethylene sheet can be used to line concrete shutters, to improve the finish of the concrete and increase the number of shutter uses, to reduce striking time and to improve the curing. The sheet can be damaged however by poker vibrators when the concrete is internally vibrated. External vibration of the concrete in beams, and tamping of the concrete in slabs is therefore preferred. It is difficult to prevent some air from being trapped beneath wrinkles in the sheet and this may disfigure the concrete surfaces.

(ii) *Nylon coatings for steel shutters*

Steel shutters sprayed with nylon improve the concrete surface; the nylon coating also protects the shutter.

(iii) *Resin-impregnated plywood*

Shuttering plywood, impregnated with phenolic resins during manufacture, can be obtained; alternatively, untreated plywood can be painted with an epoxy resin-based compound. Plywood treated in either of these ways offers greater resistance to splintering and rot. It also has more uses than untreated plywood, and enables a better finish to be obtained on the concrete. Certain types of epoxy-resin based compounds are oil filled; the oil "bleeds" after application, thus eliminating the use of mould oil.

(iv) *Glass-reinforced plastics forms*

Complete forms can be manufactured from glass-reinforced plastics for in-situ or precast concrete. They can be made self-supporting or, in the case of formwork for larger concrete units, be provided with a frame of steelwork or timber. If properly cleaned after use, they can be used several hundred times before being discarded. The resins in glass-reinforced plastics are thermo-setting, and the forms are therefore suitable where steam or heat is used to accelerate the curing of concrete. Epoxy resins are better than polyester resins however where steam is used for curing.

(v) *Polypropylene preformed moulds*

Injection moulded polypropylene pre-formed moulds are employed to produce coffered ceiling effects. They are easy to handle, erect and dismantle.

Fig. 13/3 Polypropylene preformed moulds in position before concreting (see also Fig. 12/8).

They can also be used many times, (being released by a puff of air through a specially prepared boss) and leave a smooth finish but with noticeable junctions. Moulds are made in standard modules to suit different loading and floor spans and are designed for loads up to 490 kg/m^2 on spans of up to 13-m. This type of preformed mould is illustrated in Fig. 13/3, the general arrangement and method of support being depicted in Figs. 13/4 and 13/5.

(vi) *Surface finishes*

Sculptured effects can also be obtained on the moulded surface of concrete by using moulds of carved cellular plastics or vacuum foamed sheet or glass-reinforced plastic (see also sub-section (e) on page 126).

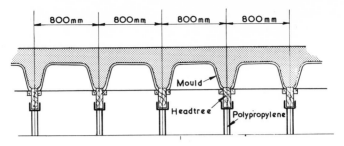

Fig. 13/4 General arrangement of moulds for Fig. 13/3.

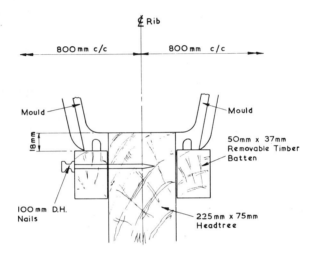

Fig. 13/5 Detail showing method of supporting moulds of Figs. 13/3 and 13/4.

(h) Curing Membranes

(i) *Use of plastics sheets*

Plastics sheets can be employed to cover new-placed concrete to assist curing by preventing excessive evaporation of water. They are cheap and light and can easily be placed in position without disturbing the surface of the concrete.

(ii) *Liquid plastics spraying*

Similar effects (to those in (i)) can be obtained by spraying plastics as a liquid on to the surface of concrete after the initial set has taken place. Silicone-based materials are usually employed, the resulting film on the concrete surface being less susceptible to damage by wind and traffic than plastics sheets. The sprayed coatings act as an effective moisture barrier for several months, even on trafficked surfaces, but will weather off in time. They are not recommended if a further surface requiring a bond is to be applied to the concrete, (unless special methods such as mechanical cleaning of the concrete surface are adopted).

(j) Tools (and accessories)

Many tools and accessories are made wholly or partly from plastics. Polyethylene, polypropylene, nylon, acrylonitrile-butodiene-styrene (ABS), plasticised polyvinyl chloride (PVC) and glass-reinforced plastics are all used in different applications to suit their particular properties, the main advantages of such materials being, lightness, corrosion resistance, ease of cleaning and quietness in use.

Typical applications, where plastics show advantage over coventional materials, include: wheelbarrows of glass-reinforced plastics, polyethylene or rubber buckets, as well as tool handles of nylon and similar plastics.

Transparent PVC and polyethylene is particularly useful as protective covers for drawings, etc., that have to be used out of doors.

"Double-insulation" has helped to make portable electric tools safer, and the use of plastics materials for such insulating purposes has played an effective part in this.

(k) Ropes

Ropes are used for many purposes in temporary work and construction plants. Some plastics ropes are superior to those made from natural fibres, and their properties can be used to advantage in certain instances. The costs of plastics ropes varies with the polymer used, but in general, the cheapest plastics rope is dearer than a natural fibre rope of the same diameter. Plastics ropes however are normally stronger than fibre ropes, and it is only after an assessment of other properties such as stretch, resistance to rot, weight, method of attachment and so forth, that a correct selection can be made.

(i) *Materials*

Plastics ropes are generally made from nylon, polyester, polypropylene or polyethylene. Nylon and polyester ropes are the more expensive, but are usually stronger. Unlike those made from natural fibres, plastics ropes are produced from continuous-spun filaments or fibrilated yarn, which combined with the properties of the polymer, gives them different handling characteristics.

(ii) *Properties*

Plastics ropes are generally lighter than natural-fibre ropes; they deteriorate less when exposed to saturation conditions and also offer good resistance to chemical attack. Their stretch properties vary however: nylon is recommended for maximum stretch but polyester is better if minimum stretch is required. Unlike those of natural fibre, plastics ropes do not shrink or stretch in wet and dry conditions.

(iii) *Using plastics ropes*

The ends of plastics ropes can be prevented from fraying by a simple heat-melting process. The thermoplastic properties of such ropes limit their use in certain instances however, and with turn binding (i.e. making a turn or loop around some suitable member to help take the load), excessive friction has been known to cause the rope to melt.

Knots used for natural-fibre ropes are not always suitable for securing plastics ropes and it is essential to comply with manufacturer's recommendations in this respect.

(l) Forming Pockets in Concrete

Reference is made in Section Three: 'Foundations' to the use of expanded polystyrene as formers for holes and pockets in concrete. This material is cheap, easily worked, and particularly suitable for forming recesses with projections perpendicular to the line of withdrawal of the former. Removal of wooden formers in these conditions can be difficult, but expanded polystyrene is easily removed by cutting out or burning. Polystyrene blocks employed to form holes for holding-down bolts can be left in position until the hole is required. This avoids the need for temporary filling and the sealing of holes to prevent cracking of the concrete from water freezing in the holes — it also prevents dirt from accumulating in the holes.

(m) Protective Clothing

It is becoming increasingly important to reduce delays in construction caused by bad weather. Clothing made from fabric-reinforced plasticised polyvinyl chloride (PVC) provides good protection against rain and wind. Jackets and trousers from these materials are generally lighter and more flexible than oil-skins. Most of the safety helments now used by construction workers and others are now made from polypropylene or glass-reinforced plastics.

APPENDIX A

CHARACTERISTICS OF PLASTICS USED IN BUILDING

(a) Introduction

This appendix briefly describes some of the characteristics of the plastics materials commonly used in building. The plastics used for the manufacture of components may be compounds of polymers, fillers, stabilisers, colourants and plasticisers, so that descriptions that are true for all grades and commercial variations cannot be given. This is not unusual and applies to other materials as well as to plastics. Thus if wood is to be used, questions of type and grade also arise — and so with plastics. Many such questions have been already answered by component manufacturers, but a knowledge of the general characteristics of a material is always useful since it can enable a builder or engineer to identify the material used, so preventing the misuse of components in service or during installation. There are however no cheap, certain ways of identifying plastics, but some knowledge of the common materials used and the types of articles or components made from them can help correct decisions to be made.

The materials are described below in the order to which most of them are referred in Table 1/2 (Section One).

(b) Thermoplastic Materials

1. *Polyvinyl chloride (PVC)*

Polyvinyl chloride, known as PVC or vinyl, is the plastics material most used in building. The polymer can be compounded to give compositions varying from the hard, rigid material used in water pipes, to the soft material used as coating on vinyl upholstery. This wide range of properties is obtained, not by varying the properties of the base polymer but by varying the additives (such as stabilisers, fillers, plasticisers), compounded with the base polymer to produce the plastics raw material. The plasticiser itself has the greatest effect and it is for this reason that PVC has such a wide range of grades and can be used in so many ways.

Rigid (unplasticised) PVC is used as pipes for water, drainage, soil, ventilation and chemical plant; as sheet for roofing, wall cladding and shutter lining; also as special profile extrusion for weather boarding, roof trims, skirting boards and electrical conduits. In this form it is hard, strong and rigid, and while generally opaque, can be transparent c.f. roofing sheet. Other compositions, containing large proportions of fillers and plasticisers, are used for floor tiles and sheet, decorative foils for walls, coatings on wall papers, insulation on electric wires, and as water stops and bars between concrete slabs.

The chemical resistance of PVC depends largely on its composition, the rigid unplasticised compound being the best. Some organic solvents attack

147

PVC moderately easily, and advantage is taken of this to produce solvent-cemented joints in pipes and roofing membranes. The resistance to weathering is generally good, but the exact effects depend on the composition of the compound and the latitude of exposure. The usual visual effect in the UK is a chalking of the surface exposed to sunlight; unexposed surfaces do not suffer so much. This chalking however has little effect on the mechanical properties of the component.

The impact resistance of rigid PVC is high at normal ambient temperatures but falls off rapidly at temperatures below 0°C. High-impact grades perform better at low temperatures. The impact resistance of plasticised grades is high because of the rubbery nature of their composition.

The mechanical properties of rigid PVC change rapidly as temperature rises. The material cannot be used continuously above 60°C, and above 80°C it becomes soft enough to be distorted easily by external forces. By compounding post-chlorinated rigid PVC with normal PVC, a compound suitable for use at temperatures up to 100°C can be produced. In fire tests, rigid PVC compositions are classed as self-extinguishing, but heavily plasticised compositions can burn. When ignited, all compositions produce a smoke and in addition to the usual products of combustion, hydrochloric acid gas is also evolved. (See Section One (c) (iii).)

2. Polyethylene (PE)

Polyethylene is the second most important thermoplastic in building and is mainly used for waterproof sheet, as damp proof membrane and damp proof course, and for pressure water pipes. The properties of polyethylene plastics also depend largely on the nature of the polymers used; they are not however modified by plasticisers, but can be influenced to a limited extent by additives such as antioxidants, colourants and fillers.

The important characteristics of the base polymers which influence the properties of polyethylene are density and melt-flow index (MFI). The first depends on the symmetry of the individual molecules, which if very symmetrical, allow easy crystallisation and, therefore, high density. Typical specific densities* range between 920 and 960 kg/m^3. The second (melt-flow index) depends on the length of the polymer chains comprising the base material. The smaller the melt-flow index, the longer the polymer chains.

Melt-flow index for common grades of polyethylene vary from 0.3 to 20, and for special grades up to 200. The following Table summarises the effects of these two factors on the properties of the polymer; the effects are not mutually exclusive and must be taken together. The third column, relating to chemical constitution, is included for completeness.

Melt-flow index is a measure of the flow properties of a polymer, and therefore reflects the ease with which a material can be processed and, in consequence, the processing costs. For normal use, a compromise between density and MFI is generally selected so as to give an optimal combination of physical properties and processing costs. In general, the low-density grades are soft and flexible, with excellent impact resistance, while the high-density grades are hard, rigid and more brittle but still tougher than many other plastics.

* See also Table 1/3.

GUIDE TO THE DEPENDENCE OF PROPERTIES OF POLYETHYLENE ON
DENSITY, MELT-FLOW INDEX (MFI) AND CHEMICAL CONSTITUENTS

(1)	(2)	(3)
MFI	*Density*	*Chemical Constitution*
As MFI decreases, the properties below increase:	As density increases, the properties below increase:	The properties below are virtually independent of MFI and density:
Tensile strength, Elongation at break, Softening point, Chemical resistance, Resistance to environmental stress cracking.	Tensile strength, Yield stress, Stiffness, Surface hardness, Softening point, Melting point,	Refractive index, Electrical properties, Thermal conductivity, Specific heat, Thermal expansion, Decomposition temperature.
As MFI decreases the property below decreases:	As density increases the property below decreases:	
Low temperature brittle point	Elongation at break	

Many properties of polyethylene are independent of density and melt-flow index, e.g. thermal expansion (which is greater than that of PVC), thermal conductivity and stability to heat and weather. Polyethylenes burn with a smokeless blue flame at a slow rate; they are not used at temperatures above about 60°C to 100°C, depending on density. They have good chemical resistance, and are not attacked by organic solvents to the extent that PVC is. Sunlight causes a breakdown of the polymer chains, with consequent deterioration of properties, though this can be prevented by additives the most effective of which is carbon black. Clear film can withstand direct exposure to sunlight for a year or so, but becomes a progressively brittle and stiff, and tears easily unless an ultraviolet stabilised grade of polymer is used. Black film maintains its properties unchanged for years.

3. *Polypropylene (PP)*

Polypropylene is not used so extensively in building as polyethylene but both have many points in common. Polypropylene is used mainly in pipe work especially for waste-water pipe, and as fittings and connectors for pitch fibre and stoneware pipes. Plastics wall tiles are also made of polypropylene.

Polypropylene, like polyethylene, belongs to the class of polymers known as polyolefines. It is a simple plastics material, the base material only being normally compounded with stabilisers, colourants and fillers. The properties depend largely on those of the base polymers, which in turn are determined by two factors, the types of polymer and their melt-flow index. Two basic types of polymers are used; those made entirely by polymerisation of propylene − (called homopolymers) − and those made by polymerisation of a mixture of propylene with a small amount of ethylene − (called copolymers).

The main difference between them is that the copolymer has a greater impact strength at low temperatures (0°C).

Melt-flow index is also a measure of the length of the molecular chains. A reduction in melt-flow index is therefore accompanied by an increase in impact strength, greater elongation and a slight reduction in stiffness; it also makes the material more difficult to process. The grades are chosen to give a balance between properties and ease of processing.

Polypropylene has mechanical properties similar to those of the high-density polyethylenes. Its temperature resistance is high, and the material can be used intermittently up to 120°C when properly stabilised. It also has good chemical resistance but is affected by direct sunlight. If intended for out-of-door use, it should (for protective reasons) incorporate stabilisers and/or pigments. The main advantages of these polymers over the closely related polyethylenes are — greater temperature resistance (provided that they have been properly stabilised) and better creep resistance. Their impact resistance at temperatures around 0°C is much poorer however, although the use of grades based on copolymers mitigates this considerably.

4. *Polystyrene (PS)*

Polystyrene is a well established plastics material in many industries, and is used for mouldings, for pipes, and in the expanded form, as thermal insulation.

Polystyrene belongs chemically to the same class of plastics as polyethylene and polypropylene, but because of its different molecular structure, its mechanical and chemical properties are quite different from those of the other polyolefines. In essence it is a non-crystalline plastics material, clear when in the pure, unfilled state; it is not however so chemically resistant as the other polyolefines. Its greatest drawback is its brittleness, and many modifications have been made in the base polymer as well as in the compounding to overcome this. As a result, there are a variety of grades having increasing impact resistance in the order:— General-Purpose, Impact, and High-Impact — a progression achieved by adding various amounts of rubbery polymers. The need for impact-resistance grades is only necessary for moulded and extruded applications, such as W.C. cisterns, pipes and lighting fittings (luminaires). The ease of attack by solvent permits the solvent-cementing of pipes and mouldings, while use in fluorescent lighting fittings has produced grades which are resistant to the yellowing effect of ultra-violet light.

The really large use of polystyrene in building is as expanded polystyrene for thermal insulation. This general-purpose grade material is generally made from small beads; each bead is expanded by means of pentane absorbed into the polymer under the action of heat. These expanded beads are then formed into sheets, blocks, slabs and tiles by heat and gentle pressure to give the well-known white "expanded polystyrene". Other processes are also used however. The main properties of the material from a building standpoint are its high thermal insulation and compressive strength.

The chemical resistance of polystyrene to solvents is poor and its softening point is low (60°C). It burns readily with a very smoky flame and has poor weather resistance.

5. *Acrylonitrile-butadiene-styrene (ABS)*

ABS is a well established variant of polystyrene used for pipes; it has high impact resistance, and a high temperature resistance even up to temperatures of 110°C.

6. *Polymethyl methacrylate (PMMA)*

This material is one of a family of plastics known as acrylics. The best known forms in which it is available are the clear cast sheets used for advertising signs, displays, and for lighting, and the coloured opaque sheets employed for the manufacture of baths.

It is a non-crystalline polymer which can be made as optically-clear mouldings, or can be mixed with dyes or pigments to give a range of clear or opaque colours. Fillers are seldom used, and most applications generally make use of its good light transmission and excellent weathering resistance properties, especially its resistance to ultra-violet light, so destructive to many other plastics.

It is available as cast sheet or as powder for extrusion and moulding. The casting operation produces a material with long polymer chains (high molecular weight) resulting in a product with enhanced impact strength, craze resistance and temperature resistance. It can be shaped however only by simple thermo-forming methods using sheet and bar. The powder for injection moulding and extrusion has a smaller molecular weight, so that processing by these methods is possible to give products which among other properties have lower impact strengths.

Apart from clarity, the weathering resistance, (which is not affected by the method of manufacture), is the most important characteristic from a building standpoint. It has moderately good heat resistance (95°C) and when ignited will burn with a clear, smokeless flame. Flame-retardant grades are available; these burn slowly with much smoke, but have poor weathering resistance.

Other acrylic polymers are employed to some extent in building, particularly in paints, where again the high-resistance of the polymer to discolouration by sunlight is required.

(c) Thermosetting Materials

1. *Phenolics and amino plastics*

These are the most used of the thermosetting resins, and in building, they are employed as binding agents for chipboard and blockboard, and as adhesives in the manufacture of plywood and doors and structural woodwork. As laminates with paper they are widely used for decorative and working surfaces, and as moulding powders for manufacture of door furniture, W.C. seats and electrical switches and plugs.

These two resin materials are grouped together because they are part of a family of resins formed by condensation of an amine or a phenol with formaldehyde. The properties of the base resin depend on the substance condensed with formaldehyde, so that a wide range of properties can be obtained; the most used substances are urea, which gives urea-formaldehyde

(UF); melamine, which gives melamine-formaldehyde (MF), and phenol which gives phenol-formaldehyde (PF).

The resins are formed in two stages; the first produces a partly-reacted thermoplastic polymer, used directly for adhesives or binders, or is mixed with fillers such as wood flour or paper pulp to produce a moulding material. The final processing of the first stage polymer (in presses) by the action of heat or catalysts completes the chemical reaction and a rigid non-softening solid is produced. The first stage polymer melts during this process and so allows the press to form the polymer into its final shape before the thermo-setting action is complete. The phenolic-formaldehyde resins when fully thermoset are rigid, scratch resistant, will not melt and are not affected by organic solvents, although some acids or alkalis will attack them. The mechanical and other properties depend on the filler used with the resin; wood flour, paper pulp, asbestos or glass fibres, and cellulose fibres are generally used; fibrous fillers give high-impact resistance. The phenolic resins are always dark brown in colour and so the mouldings are usually brown or black. The exact composition of the resin, especially fillers, depends on the application. They are all self-extinguishing, have high heat resistance, and good electrical-insulating properties.

The properties of aminoplasts are generally similar to those of the phenolics and again depend on the fillers. The main apparent difference is that the aminos are colourless and can therefore be given bright colours. Thus, decorative laminates incorporate a phenolic resin base with layers of urea resin and melamine resin on the surface to give the decorative and wear layer respectively.

2. Unsaturated polyesters

These resins are being increasingly used as structural mouldings and as weather-cladding and roof lighting. They are generally obtained as viscous liquids which are mixed with a hardener and then "layed-up" with glass-fibre mat or woven cloth to form the final moulding shape. The hardener acts at room temperature to thermoset the resin to a hard, clear, brittle solid which because of the high content of glass fibres, has good mechanical properties, especially tensile strength and rigidity.

The mechanical properties depend on chemical composition but more on the amount of glass-reinforcement and its orientation in the moulding. The resins besides being hard and colourless offer high resistance to most organic solvents, but are attacked by alkalis and concentrated acids. They also have a good temperature resistance, the maximum temperature at which they can be used depending on their compositions. They burn with a smoky flame but can be formulated to be self-extinguishing. Their weather resistance depends on formulation but can be high, although after about ten years' exposure, a new surface coat may be required.

3. Epoxy resins

These are chemically different from unsaturated polyester resins, but are often employed for similar applications. The deciding factor is often cost, but technical considerations, such as adhesion to glass-reinforcement, and shrinkage are often crucial. They are also widely used as adhesives and as thermosetting agents in special road surfaces (e.g. over bridges) and floor screeds.

Epoxy resins are available as reactive resins (ranging from low-viscosity liquids to high-melting solids), which are cured to cross-linked infusible materials by the addition of co-reactants or catalytic hardeners. Depending on the system chosen, a cure may be effected at room temperature or at elevated temperatures. A wide choice of resins is available, including general-purpose, flexible, heat-resistant and flame-retardant grades. They can be modified with mineral fillers, fibrous reinforcement or other resinous products, to alter heat transfer, expansion coefficient or mechanical strength.

The formulated resins are handled as liquids and hot melts for adhesives, castings and mastic coatings; as finely divided or granular solids for powder coatings or mouldings; and as solutions for coatings. Because of the great number of different combinations of resin and hardener (curing agents), their physical properties can be varied widely.

4. *Polyurethanes (PUR)*

Polyurethane polymers, are made by reacting polyisocyanates with poly-hydroxyl compounds in the presence of catalysts. They can be made from a wide variety of raw materials to give hard, clear resins for surface coating; soft flexible resins for oil-resistant and abrasion resistant rubbers; rigid or flexible foams for thermal insulation, cushion and fabric stiffeners. In building, surface coating and thermal insulation are their main applications.

The flexibility range of the polymers is obtained by using different types of poly-hydroxyl compounds with the same polyisocyanate. The properties of a surface coating depend on its exact formulation, but the surfaces produced are generally very hard and scratch resistant, with good wearing properties; they are also resistant to most oils, greases, and chemicals, but not strong acids. The elastomeric rubber materials combine good oil and abrasion resistance with a long life.

The properties of the rigid foams depend more on the physical structure of the foam, and for any particular density of foam, on the cell size and cell orientation which in turn depends on the method of manufacture. A narrow distribution of cell sizes of spherical cells produces the better foams and these are obtained under controlled factory conditions. Such foams have good mechanical properties with moderate temperature resistance. In fires, they burn with a smoky flame, but self-extinguishing types are available.

APPENDIX B

BIBLIOGRAPHY AND SOME RELEVANT BRITISH STANDARDS

The publications cited below under items (a) and (b) are amongst those which since 1967 provide information relevant to the use of plastics materials in building: –

(a) BOOKS

(1) Structural Design with Plastics: B.S. Benjamin (1969): Van Nostrand Reinhold, Connecticut, U.S.A.

(2) Insulation Products: Guide to the Use of Cellular Plastics in Building (1968): British Plastics Federation, London W.1.

(3) Reinforced Plastics Conference (6th International) (1968): British Plastics Federation, London W.1.

(4) Applications and Durability of Plastics: Digest No. 69 (new series) Building Research Station, Garston, Watford, HMSO (reprint 1969).

(5) Plastics in Architecture: A. G. H. Dietz and M. E. Goody: Massachusetts Institute of Technology (1967 Summer Meeting of Department of Architecture): M.I.T. Press, Massachusetts, U.S.A.

(6) Plastics for Architects: A. G. H. Dietz (1970): M.I.T. Press, Massachusetts, U.S.A.

(7) Studies in the Field of Structural Plastics and Building Structures Based on These, Parts 1 and 2, Edited A. B. Gubenko and H. G. Allen: Translated from Russian by P. Birnbarum: National Lending Library for Science and Technology.

(8) Flammability Handbook for Plastics: C. J. Hilado (1969): Technomic Publication Company, Stanford, Connecticut, U.S.A.

(9) Plastics for Building: ICI Plastics Division Publication (1967), Welwyn Garden City, Herts.

(10) Plastics in the Building Industry: R. Reboul and R. G. B. Mitchell (1968): G. Newnes Ltd., (now Hamcyn Publishers, Manchester).

(11) Plastics in Building: Regional Technical Conference, Chicago, Oct. 1969, of Society of Plastics Engineers, Connecticut, U.S.A.

(12) Vinyls in Building: Regional Technical Conference, 1967, New York Society of Plastics Engineers, Connecticut, U.S.A.

(b) PAMPHLETS

(1) Cellular Plastics for Building, Digest No. 93 (new series): Building Research Station, Garston, Watford.

(2) Cellular Plastics for Building, Digest No. 94 (new series): Building Research Station, Garston, Watford.

(3) Plastic Trends in Building and Construction: Southern California Regional Technical Corporation (1968): Society of Plastics Engineers, Connecticut, U.S.A.

154

(c) RELEVANT BRITISH STANDARDS

Note: Reference should always be made to the latest issue of a British Standard, and to any published amendments.

B.S. 476   Fire Tests on Building Materials.

Part 1: Fire Tests on Building Materials and Structures.
Test for surface spread of flame and fire resistance of structures, with definitions of these terms in relation to building materials. Describes a method testing surface spread of flame suitable for a preliminary check.

Part 3: External Fire Exposure Roof Tests.
Method of test for sloping and flat roof specimens to ascertain penetration and spread of flame from fire in adjacent buildings.

Part 4: Non-Combustibility Tests for Materials.
Specifies tests to determine whether materials with or without coatings, used in construction or finishing of buildings meet the definition of non-combustibility.

Part 5: Ignitability Test for Materials.
Preliminary test to assess behaviour of materials in sheet or slab form when subject to a small flame.

Part 6: Fire Propagation Test for Materials.
Compares the contributions of combustible building materials to the growth of fire.

Part 7: Surface Spread of Flame Test for Materials.
Large scale test to assess the tendency of materials to support spread of flame across their surfaces, and classification.

B.S. 1331   Builders' Hardware for Housing.
Schedules of the most generally used builders hardware applicable to housing. It covers articles in iron, steel, non-ferrous metals and plastics.

B.S. 1334   The Use of Thermal Insulating Materials for Central Heating and Hot and Cold Water Supply Installations.
Specifies minimum thicknesses of insulating material for heat conservation or for frost protection. Appendices describe methods of calculation.

B.S. 1755   Glossary of Terms Used in the Plastics Industry.
(Being   Lists some 450 terms grouped into six sections, chemistry,
revised   properties, industrial applications, moulding processes, con-
and issued   stituents, other manufacturing processes.
in Parts, as (Part 1: Polymerization and Plastics Materials)
from 1967)

B.S. 2050   Electrical Resistance of Conductive and Anti-Static Products Made From Flexible Polymeric Material.
Specifies the limits of electrical resistance of anti-static and conductive articles and products including those for hospital use, tyres and belting.

B.S. 2782   Methods of Testing Plastics.
Specifies tests for temperature effects, electrical properties, mechanical properties.

B.S. 3502   Schedule of Common Names and Abbreviations for Plastics and Rubbers.

B.S. 3532   Unsaturated Polyester Resin Systems for Low Pressure Fibre
                 Reinforced Plastics.
                 Specifies five types of material classified by deflection temper-
                 ature of cast resin under load.

B.S. 3534   Epoxide Resin Systems for Glass Fibre-Reinforced Plastics.
                 Part 1: 1962 Wet lay-up systems.
                 Part 2: 1964 Pre-impregnation systems.

(d) BRITISH STANDARDS RELATING TO SECTION FOUR: EXTERNAL WALLS, DOORS, ROOFS AND WINDOWS

B.S. 476   Part 3: External Fire Exposure Roof Tests.
                 Method of test for sloping and flat roof specimens to ascertain
                 penetration and spread of flame from fire in adjacent
                 buildings.

B.S. 743   Materials for Damp-Proof Courses.
                 Selection and laying of damp-proof courses; composition of
                 mortar for bedding or laying of courses, and for bedding bricks
                 and slates as damp-proof courses. Includes the use of plastics
                 materials such as polythene film.

B.S. 1755   Glossary of Terms Used in the Plastics Industry.

B.S. 2552   Polystyrene Tiles for Walls and Ceilings.

B.S. 3932   Expanded Polystyrene Tiles and Profiles for the Building Industry.

B.S. 4154   Corrugated Plastics Translucent Sheeting Made From Thermo-
                 setting Polyester Resins (Glass-Fibre Reinforced).

B.S. 4203   Extruded Rigid PVC Corrugated Sheeting.

(e) BRITISH STANDARDS RELATING TO SECTION FIVE: CEILINGS, AND SECTION SIX: PARTITIONS

B.S. 1763   Thin PVC Sheeting (Flexible, Unsupported).
                 Nominal thickness 0.002-in to 0.015-in in following types:
                 Type 1 G.P. unprinted single with plain or embossed surface.
                 Type 2 Thin sheeting of type 1, printed.
                 Type 1F Thin sheeting of type 1, flame resistant.
                 Type 2F Thin sheeting of type 1F, printed.

B.S. 1811   Methods of Test for Wood Chipboards and Other Particle Boards.
                 Part 1: 1961 Imperial Units.
                 Part 2: 1969 Metric Units.

B.S. 2604   Resin-bonded Wood Chipboard. (Part 1 withdrawn; Part 2, Metric Units)
                 Specifies requirements for the properties of wood chipboard
                 (For test methods see B.S. 1811).

B.S. 2739   Thick PVC Sheeting (Flexible, Unsupported).
                 General purpose calendered single or laminated sheeting with
                 plain or embossed surface in the nominal thickness range
                 0.010-in to 0.035-in inclusive.

B.S. 3012   Low-Density Polythene Sheet.
                   Specifies black, natural, pink and brown sheet in two grades of
                   polymer.

B.S. 3757   Rigid PVC Sheet.
                   Part 1: Pressed sheet.
                   Describes four types of pressed sheet in a range of thicknesses.
                   Part 2: Calendered and extruded sheet.
                   Describes four types of calendered or extruded sheet in a range
                   of thicknesses.

B.S. 3835   Rigid PVC Profiles for Fitting Sheet Lining Materials.
                   Covers rigid PVC profiles for Grade A1 and Grade B PVC
                   Compound (B.S. 3168).

B.S. 3837   Expanded Polystyrene Board for Thermal Insulation Purposes.

B.S. 3869   Rigid Expanded PVC for Thermal Insulation Purposes and
                   Building Applications.
                   Covers block, board and sheet for thermal insulation up to
                   50°C.

B.S. 3932   Expanded Polystyrene Tiles and Profiles for the Building Industry.
                   Covers moulded, cut and machined expanded polystyrene of
                   nominal apparent density.

B.S. 4154   Corrugated Plastics Translucent Sheets Made from Thermosetting
                   Polyester Resins (Glass Fibre-Reinforced).
                   Specifies dimensions, tolerances, strengths, light transmission
                   and the fire hazard of GRP translucent sheet.

B.S. 4203   Extruded Rigid PVC Corrugated Sheeting.
                   Specifies colour fastness, dimensions, tolerances, strength and
                   light transmission of rigid corrugated sheet.

(f) BRITISH STANDARDS RELATING TO SECTION SEVEN: FLOORING

C.P. 203   Sheet and Tile Flooring (Cork, Linoleum, Plastics and Rubber).
                   Gives recommendations for selection, laying and maintenance
                   of tiles.

B.S. 2552   Polystyrene Tiles for Walls and Ceilings.
                   Specifies dimensions, materials, opacity, colour fastness and
                   workmanship, requirements for adhesive.

B.S. 2592   Thermoplastic Flooring Tiles (Sometimes known as "Asphalt"
                   Tiles).
                   Specifies material, dimensions, colour, quality and mechanical
                   tests for a type of tile for use of rigid sub-floors.

B.S. 3260   PVC (Vinyl) Asbestos Floor Tiles. (Metric and Imperial Units.)
                   Specifies dimensions and physical characteristics of smooth
                   surfaced homogeneous floor tiles.

B.S. 3261   Flexible PVC Flooring.
                   Covers materials supplied in continuous lengths or in tile form,
                   with or without hessian backing.

(g) BRITISH STANDARDS RELATING TO SECTION EIGHT: SERVICES

B.S. 546	Two-Pole and Earthing-Pin Plugs, Socket-Outlets and Socket-Outlet Adaptors for Circuits up to 250 Volts.
B.S. 1212	Ballvalves (Plymouth Type) Excluding Floats.
B.S. 1363	13 A Plugs, Switched and Unswitched Socket-Outlets and Boxes.
B.S. 1972	Polythene Pipe (Type 32) for Cold Water Services.
B.S. 1973	Polythene Pipe (Type 425) for General Purposes Including Chemical and Food Industry Uses.
B.S. 2004	PVC-Insulated Cables and Flexible Cords for Electric Power and Lighting.
B.S. 2456	Floats for Ballvalves (Plastics) for Cold Water.
B.S. 3284	Polythene Pipe (Type 50) for Cold Water Services.
B.S. 3505	Unplasticised PVC Pipe for Cold Water Services.
B.S. 3506	Unplasticised PVC Pipe for Industrial Purposes.
B.S. 3796	Polythene Pipe (Type 710) for General Purposes Including Chemical and Food Industry Uses.
B.S. 3867	Outside Diameters and Pressure Ratings of Pipe of Plastics Materials.
B.S. 3943	Plastics Waste Traps.
B.S. 4213	Polyolefine or Olefine Copolymer Moulded Cold Water Storage Cisterns.
B.S. 4346	Joints and Fittings for Use With Unplasticised PVC Pressure Pipes. Part 1: Injection Moulded UPVC Fittings for Solvent Welding for Use with Pressure Pipes Including Potable Water Supply. Part 2: Mechanical Joints and Fittings Principally of Unplasticised PVC.
B.S. 4375	Unsintered PTFE Tape for Thread Sealing Applications.
B.S. 4514	Unplasticised PVC Soil and Ventilating Pipe, Fittings and Accessories.
B.S. 4576	Unplasticised PVC Rainwater Goods. Part 1: 1970 Half-round Gutters and Circular Pipes.
B.S. 4607	Non-Metallic Conduits and Fittings for Electrical Installations. Part 1: Rigid PVC Conduits and Conduit Fittings, Metric Units, Part 2: Imperial Units.
B.S. 4660	Unplasticised PVC Underground Drain Pipe and Fittings.
B.S. 6004	PVC-Insulated Cables (Non-Armoured) for Electric Power and Lighting (Metric).
B.S. 6234	Polythene Insulation and Sheath for Electric Cables.
B.S. 6346	PVC-Insulated Cables for Electricity Supply.
B.S. 6746	PVC-Insulation and Sheath for Electric Cables.

(h) BRITISH STANDARDS RELEVANT TO SECTION NINE: JOINTING AND SEALANTS, SECTION TEN: ADHESIVES AND SECTION ELEVEN: ADDITIVES

B.S. 1203	Synthetic Resin Adhesives for Plywood.
B.S. 1204	Synthetic Resin Adhesives for Wood.
B.S. 3544	Methods of Test for Polyvinyl Acetate Adhesives for Wood. Specifies tests for staining, strength of lap joints and freeze/thaw resistance.
B.S. 3712	Methods of Test for Building Mastics (Other than Mastic Asphalt).
B.S. 4071	Polyvinyl Acetate (PVA) Emulsion Adhesives for Wood.
B.S. 4254	Two-Part Polysulphide-Based Sealing Compounds for the Building Industry.

(j) BRITISH STANDARD RELEVANT TO SECTION TWELVE: BUILDING ACCESSORIES

B.S. 1125	W.C. Flushing Cisterns (Including Dual Flush Cisterns and Flush Pipes). Covers requirements for materials, workmanship, certain design features, construction, dimensions, performance and working of W.C. flushing cisterns of the "2 gallon" type and the "1 or 2 gallon" (dual flush) type.
B.S. 1254	W.C. Seats (Plastics)
B.S. 1876	Automatic Flushing Cisterns for Urinals. Specifies requirements, suitable materials and construction.
B.S. 4135	Sinks for Domestic Purposes, Made from Cast Acrylic Sheet. Specifies dimensions and constructional requirements.
B.S. 4305	Baths for Domestic Purposes Made from Cast Acrylic Sheet. Specifies properties of cast sheet from which two types of bath are made. Design, dimensions and construction features are covered.
B.S. 4375	Unsintered PTFE Tape for Thread Sealing Applications. Specifies composition, lubricant, thread wrapping and sealing properties, width, thickness and test methods.

(k) OTHER PUBLICATIONS

Note: Items 1 and 2 are relevant to Section Eight of this Handbook, and items 3 to 5 inclusive to Sections Nine, Ten and Eleven.

(1) Thermoplastics Pipework and Ducting in Unplasticised Polyvinyl Chloride, EEUA Handbook No. 20 (1965). Constable and Co. Ltd., London W.C.2.

(2) Guide to Installation of Unplasticised PVC Soil Pipe Systems; Institute of Plumbing (1970), Scottish Mutual House, North Street, Hornchurch, Essex.

(3) Adhesives Used in Building: Advisory Leaflet No. 77 (1969), Ministry of Public Buildings and Works. H.M. Stationery Office.

(4) Manual of Application for Two-Part Polysulphide Sealants (prepared by Sealant Manufacturers Conference); British Rubber Manufacturers Association Ltd., 9, Whitehall, London, S.W.1.

(5) Sealants: M. Garrido, Design Engineering, Summit House, Gleebe Way, West Wickham, Kent.

(6) Series on Plastics in Building (Insulation Products, Corrugated Plastics Sheets, Resin-Bonded Chip Board, Plastics-Surfaced Sheet Material, Pipes and Pipework) British Plastics Federation, 47–48 Piccadilly, London. W.1.

APPENDIX C

IMPERIAL/METRIC (SI) EQUIVALENTS

Imperial	Metric
1 in	25.4 mm
1 in^2	645.16 mm^2
1 UK Gal	4.546 litre
1 US Gal	3.785 litre
1 lb	0.4536 kg
1 lbf/in^2	6.8948 kN/m^2 = 6.8948 x 10^{-2} bar
1 lbf	4.4482 N
1 Std. Atmosphere	1.013 bar
3 lbf/in^2	20 kN/m^2 = 0.2 bar
15 lbf/in^2	0.1 MN/m^2 = 1.0 bar ($\approx$ 1 atmos)
300 lbf/in^2	2.0 MN/m^2
1 tonf/ft^2	0.1 MN/m^2
1 tonf/in^2	15 MN/m^2
1 joule	(1 newton x 1 metre) $\doteq$ 1 N m
1 watt	1 N m/s
1 Btu	1.055 kJ
1 kcal	4.1868 kJ
1 Btu/ft^2 h $^\circ$F. (thermal conductance)	5.6783 W/m^2 $^\circ$C (= "U" Value)
1 Btu in/ft^2 h $^\circ$F. (thermal conductivity)	0.1442 W/m $^\circ$C (= "k" Value)

Note: regarding units for pressure and stress.
B.S.I. recommendations on the units for pressure and stress are: –

(a) For stress use N/m^2 (and multiples) *or* N/mm^2.
(b) For pressure use N/m^2 (and multiples) *or* bar (or mbar).
(c) Pressures or differentials may be stated as a height of a specified fluid, subject to appropriate conversions.
(d) Where distinction is necessary "gauge pressure" or "absolute pressure" should be specified.

At present it seems that the newton per square metre (N/m^2) will be known internationally as the pascal (Pa).

ACKNOWLEDGEMENTS

The Association wishes to thank all those who took part or helped in the preparation of this Handbook, including those who supplied information on recent developments or who provided data for assessment by the Panel. Thanks are also extended to the following firms for permission to make use of or to reproduce certain data or illustrations:—

Acalor (1848) Limited, Crawley, Sussex.
Anderson (D) and Son Limited, Manchester.
Armitage Ware Limited, Armitage, Staffs.

Brady (G) and Company Limited, Manchester.
Brand Coatings Limited, Letchworth, Herts.
British Celanese Limited, Coventry, Warwickshire.
British Plastics Federation, London, W.1.
Brocks Ventilation Units Limited, Croydon, Sussex.

Carron Company Limited, Falkirk, Stirlingshire.
Cement and Concrete Association, London, S.W.1.
Crittall Hope Limited, Braintree, Essex.

Duplos Domes Limited, Leicester.
Dynamit Nobel A. G. Cologne, Germany.

English Electric Company Limited, Preston, Lancashire.

Fetim N. V, Amsterdam, Holland.
Franco British Electrical Company Limited, London, S.W.1.

Glasdon Limited, Blackpool, Lancashire.

Hepworth Iron Company Limited, Sheffield, Yorkshire.
Honeywell Controls Limited, Watford, Hertfordshire.
Hope (H) and Son, Smethwick, Staffordshire.

IMI Developments Limited, Birmingham.
Isora Integrated Ceilings Limited, Slough, Bucks.

Kaiser Floors Limited, Maidenhead, Berkshire.
Key Terrain Limited, Maidstone, Kent.
Koninklije Fabrick, F. W. Bratt N. V., Delft, Holland.

Ministry of Public Buildings and Works Research Station, Garston, Watford.
Monsanto Chemicals Limited, London, S.W.1.
Monza Fensterbau GmbH and Company, Hessen, Germany.

Osma Plastics Limited, Hayes, Middlesex.

Plastics Constructions Limited, Birmingham.
Plastidrain Limited, Burnley, Lancashire.

Rehau Plastics GmbH, Rehau, Germany.
Royds Manchester Limited, Manchester.

Sandford-Brysson Limited, London, S.W.1.
Scott-Bader Services Limited, Northampton.

Transplastix Limited, Newcastle, England.

Youngman System Buildings Limited. Crawley, Sussex.